ENGLISH PAPER MONEY

The 1914 Bank of England £1

The Bank of England £1 note of 1914, in its proof form above, ranks as one of the major rarities of the English series. It had been assumed that the only extant copy was held by the Bank itself, until three further specimens came on to the market in 1974 from the effects of a former Bank of England Governor. One of these was sold at auction on 7 June 1975 by Stanley Gibbons Currency Ltd for £1200.

The history of the note is bound up with the currency crisis at the outbreak of the First World War in August 1914. It had become increasingly clear during the summer to both Treasury and Bank of England officials that some form of paper money of a lower denomination than £5 would have to be substituted for the gold sovereign. The question was who would issue it.

The Bank of England had no doubts about its claim and made preparations accordingly. Indeed, it was not until the "rival" Treasury notes (T1 to T10) were actually being printed that the Chancellor of the Exchequer, Lloyd George, revealed his hand at a meeting with leading bankers on 5 August, a few hours after war had been declared.

The critical point about the new notes—which had apparently escaped the Government—was their convertibility into gold, and hence their acceptability to the public. Only after a heated discussion was a formula agreed whereby Treasury notes should be convertible, but only at the Bank of England itself, and not at any other bank.

The guarantee on the historic Bank of England £1 shows an awareness of reality and a sense of monetary discipline sadly lacking in today's inflationary climate.

ENGLISH PAPER MONEY

Vincent Duggleby

Stanley Gibbons Publications Ltd
391 Strand, London WC2R 0LX

By Appointment to Her Majesty The Queen
Stanley Gibbons Ltd, Philatelists

© Stanley Gibbons Publications Ltd 1975

First published 1975

ISBN 0 85259 790 8

Printed in Great Britain by
William Clowes & Sons Limited, London, Colchester and Beccles

Preface

In Britain the new collector of English paper money will find that he can make a good start by examining the banknotes in his wallet. Apart from various denominations there are likely to be several different signatures. Check to see if the banknotes are misprints; sometimes the serial numbers on each note do not match. Make sure the prefix coding is normal: there are scarce prefix codings which add substantially to the value. They are listed in this catalogue.

O'Brien signature £1 notes are occasionally found in circulation. Check the backs to see if a little "R" occupies the space above the framed "Bank of England" on the lower left side: it is a rarity. "G" notes are worth looking for too; the letter is in the same position on Hollom and Fforde notes as the "R" on O'Brien notes, but they are found more frequently. There are many slight differences in British banknotes which make them desirable notaphilic items.

Apart from the notes dealt with in this catalogue there is a wide range of British private banknotes, most of which are no longer valid. Several hundred different Banks can be collected. Scotland has the widest range of notes available and even a "one of each" collection becomes quite large. Until recently numerous Scottish banks issued notes and even today, unlike England, several different banks make note issues. A full priced catalogue listing will be found in James Douglas's *Scottish Banknotes* (from the same publisher as the present work).

It is hoped that the new collector will find of assistance in his studies the general information at the end of this book. Likewise the research findings embodied throughout the text should be of benefit to the more experienced collector wanting a reliable and up-to-date guide to the fascinating world of English paper money.

London   VINCENT DUGGLEBY

Acknowledgements

The author expresses his thanks to the following organisations for assistance given during the compilation of this book:
The Inland Revenue (particularly the Director of Stamping).
The Public Record Office.
The British Museum.
H.M. Treasury.
The Bank of England (who have kindly sanctioned publication).
Apart from countless members of the International Bank Note Society, several other individuals have been particularly helpful, too, including David Keable, Colin Narbeth and editorial staff at Stanley Gibbons, and to these the author is most grateful.

Catalogue Terms

Obverse

Front of a banknote.

Reverse

Back of a banknote.

Prefix

The combination of letters and numbers that precede the actual serial number, e.g. on Bank of England notes:
   X41 (= letter, number, number)
   28A (= number, number, letter)
   R31L (= letter, number, number, letter)
   AN64 (= letter, letter, number, number)
On Treasury notes the prefixes most usually found are:
   $\frac{B}{41}$ (= letter over number)
   $\frac{F1}{8}$ $\frac{H2}{23}$ (= letter and figure over number)

Dot

A variety found on some Treasury notes where the prefix "No" has a full stop after or under it. In some cases this is normal, in others it is a variety.

Dash

As above but a dash instead of a full stop. This may also be referred to as a "square dot" variety.

Metal thread

The "thread" or metal filament inserted into the paper of modern Bank of England notes which shows up clearly when the note is held up to the light.

Illustrations

Illustrations of single notes in this catalogue are ½ linear size.

Colours of notes

Generally only the predominant colours are given in the lists.

Prices

Banknotes have been priced for Very Fine (VF) condition to 1914 and thereafter for Very Fine and Extremely Fine (EF) conditions. They are available with or without specified serial prefix. It should be remembered that many of them can be obtained for very much less in worn condition; 100% uncirculated notes cost more. For information on how to grade condition *see* page 106.

In the price columns:
- Exists but no price can be quoted.
* Not yet identified, so no price can be quoted.
† Readily obtained from circulation.

Contents

Contents

Treasury Notes

In 1914 the gold sovereign and half-sovereign were used as everyday currency. With the advent of war the Treasury acted quickly to produce £1 and 10s. notes to meet the expected gold-hoarding.

Under the 1833 Act, Bank of England notes were legal tender in England and Wales only for amounts of over £5. The 1914 Currency and Bank Notes Act, passed on 5 August (the day after war was declared), empowered the Treasury to issue currency notes and gave them full legal tender status. The Bank of England had no reason to be pleased about this and, in fact, in July 1914 had prepared designs for Bank of England £1 banknotes (*see* Frontispiece).

The Treasury officials decided to use their own notes which were, however, badly and hurriedly designed. The August Bank Holiday was extended for three clear days to allow the Treasury to rush through the printing of the notes. At the time there were not sufficient stocks of banknote paper so the Treasury used stamp paper. The first issue of Treasury notes bears the Royal Cypher ("Simple") watermark as do the postage stamps of that period. Even so, the shortage of paper money led to postal orders being allowed to pass for legal tender for a few weeks.

The Treasury notes were signed by Sir John Bradbury, Permanent Secretary to the Treasury, and measured only 5 by 2½ inches. They were quickly nicknamed "Bradburys". A week later a 10s. note was also introduced.

In October 1914 the Treasury £1 notes were replaced by a new and more carefully engraved design by George Eve, who had designed some of the postage stamps. The 10s. note appeared in 1915. These second-issue notes, which were printed on proper banknote paper, were larger than the first. Then in February 1917 a third design by Bertram Mackennal—the man responsible for the coinage of George V—appeared on £1 notes. This featured a vignette of St. George and the Dragon on the obverse and the Houses of Parliament on the reverse. In November 1918 new 10s. notes, with a vignette of Britannia standing, were issued.

When Sir Warren Fisher succeeded Bradbury at the Treasury, the same designs were used but with Warren Fisher signatures. In 1928 there was an alteration to the wording on the notes, when the word NORTHERN was added to IRELAND following recognition of the partition.

In 1918, following persistent reports of silver-hoarding, particularly in Ireland, designs and plates were prepared for small-denomination notes of

5s, 2s.6d. and 1s. The 5s. notes were printed with Bradbury's signature, but were never issued. All three denominations, however, were printed on the authority of Fisher and although these, too, were not officially issued, a few specimens slipped out.

Treasury notes ceased to be issued in November 1928, when the Bank of England took over responsibility for redeeming the issue. It was withdrawn on 1 August 1933.

1. John Bradbury (First Baron Bradbury) (1872–1950)

Entered the Civil Service in 1896, first the Colonial Office and then the Treasury. After serving under Asquith and then Lloyd George (including help with the famous Budget of 1909), Bradbury was appointed one of two permanent Secretaries of the Treasury in 1913 (along with Sir Thomas Heath). On the outbreak of the First World War, Bradbury quickly realised the necessity of replacing gold with paper currency, and the banknotes which were issued carried his signature; they were immediately nicknamed "Bradburys". He remained the Government's chief financial adviser during the War, eventually leaving the Treasury on 27 August 1919 to become principal British delegate to the Reparation Commission. He was knighted in 1913 and created a peer in January 1925.

First Issue

1914 (7 August) ONE POUND
Emergency issue authorised by H.M. Government and designed at the Royal Mint. Surface-printed in sheets of 36 (4 × 9) on one side only by Waterlow Bros. and Layton from plates by Eyre and Spottiswoode, on ordinary stamp paper with watermark of the Royal Cypher ("Simple") and the word or part of the word POSTAGE. First-issue Treasury notes measure 127 × 63·5 mm (5 × 2½ in.) and were legal tender until 12 June 1920. The first two and a half million notes, which were delivered to the banks on Thursday, 6 August, for issue the following morning, can be identified by the large capital A, B or C prefix (*see* T1 and T2).

Price

EF   VF

T1   £1   Black on white
Prefix coding: Single capital letter A., B. or
C. and six-digit serial number.
Quantity printed: 2½ million.

T1

		EF	VF
Serial letters:			
A		£100	50·00
B		85·00	45·00
C		£105	55·00

T2 £1 Black on white
As T1 but with full stop omitted after serial letters.

Serial letters:		EF	VF
A		£100	50·00
B		85·00	45·00
C		£105	55·00

T1 (and its variety T2) can rightly be described as the "first modern British banknotes".

T3 £1 Black on white 85·00 40·00
Prefix coding: Letter over number ("dot") and six digits.
Quantity printed: Not known.
Serial letters:
A to Z (not inclusive)

T4 £1 Black on white 85·00 40·00
As T3 but with five-digit serial number.

T5 £1 Black on white 85·00 40·00
As T3 but with "dash" and five digits.

T6 £1 Black on white 85·00 40·00
As T3 but prefix coding is double letter over number.

T7 £1 Black on white 90·00 45·00
As T3 but much smaller typeface is used.

Due to the practice of printing some additional notes down the sheet margin (*see* illustration on page 4) most of the above can be found with

BRADBURY (contd.)

Additional notes printed at edge of sheet of First Issue £1

watermark sideways (add 25% to above prices). The watermark is also found inverted and sideways inverted (add 50%).

$$\text{A } 754774$$
T2

$$\overset{S}{_{32}}\text{N}\underline{\text{o}}\ 062350$$
T3

$$\overset{J}{_{20}}\text{N}\underline{\text{o}}\ 75530$$
T4

$$\overset{K}{_{20}}\text{N}\underline{\text{o}}\ 39217$$
T5

$$\overset{DD}{_{26}}\text{N}\underline{\text{o}}\ 012471$$
T6

$$\overset{D}{_{18}}\text{N}\underline{\text{o}}\ 003659$$
T7

(The above examples are not reproduced from actual notes but are set in similar typefaces to facilitate identification.)

Note—Some people have queried the possibility that notes with five digits, which are the hallmark of De La Rue, might in fact have been printed by that company. There is no evidence to support this, but in the absence of any records it is possible that bundles of printed notes might have been sent to them for numbering only.

1914 (14 August) TEN SHILLINGS

Emergency issue authorised by H.M. Government and designed at the Royal Mint. Surface-printed in sheets of 36 (4 × 9) on one side only by Waterlow Bros. and Layton (T8 and T9) and by De La Rue and Co. (T10) on ordinary stamp paper as the £1 above. Dimensions and legal tender also as £1 above.

			Price	
			EF	VF
T8	10s.	Red on white	90·00	45·00
		Prefix coding: Letter over number ("dot") and six digits.		
		Quantity printed: Not known.		
		Serial letters: A to Z (not inclusive)		
T9	10s.	Red on white	80·00	40·00
		As T8 but the word "No" is set in different type and precedes the prefix coding.		
		Quantity printed: Not known.		
		Serial letters: A to Z (not inclusive)		

T9

BRADBURY (contd.)

Price

	EF	VF

T10 10s.　Red on white　　　　　　　　　　80·00　　40·00
Prefix coding: Letter over number ("dot")
and five digits.
Quantity printed: Not known.
Serial letters:
A to Z (not inclusive)

As with the £1 some additional notes were printed in the sheet margin and the above can be found with watermark sideways (add 25% to above prices). The watermark is also found inverted and sideways inverted (add 50%).

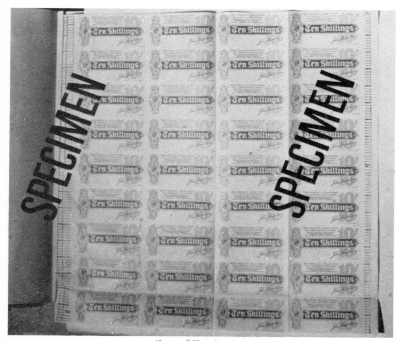

Sheet of First Issue 10s.

$^{D}_{25}$ N⁰ 747283

T8 (Waterlow Bros.)

$^{B}_{71}$ N⁰ 32557

T10 (De La Rue)

(The above examples are not reproduced from actual notes but are set in similar typeface to facilitate identification.)

Second Issue

1914 (23 October) ONE POUND
Designed by George Eve. Surface-printed in sheets of 30 (5 × 6) on one side only by De La Rue and Co. on banknote paper manufactured by William Joynson and Co. with watermark of wavy lines incorporating the Royal Cypher, the ONE POUND denomination and the four British emblems: rose, thistle, shamrock and daffodil. Second-issue Treasury £1 notes measure 149 × 83 mm (5⅞ × 3¼ in.) and were legal tender until 12 June 1920.

			Price	
			EF	VF
T11 £1	Black on white		55·00	30·00

Prefix coding:
Type 1: Letter over number and five digits
Type 2: Letter and figure "1" over number and five digits
Type 3: Letter and figure "2" over number and five digits
Quantity printed: Not known.
Serial letters:
A to Z (possibly not inclusive)

T11 Type 2

1915 (21 January) TEN SHILLINGS
Designed by George Eve. Surface-printed in sheets of 30 (5 × 6) on one side only by De La Rue and Co. (T12) and by Waterlow Bros. and Layton (T13) on banknote paper manufactured by William Joynson and Co. as the £1 above. Second-issue Treasury 10s. notes measure 136 × 76 mm (5⅜ × 3 in.) and were legal tender until 12 June 1920.

BRADBURY (*contd.*)

T12 Type 3

	Price	
	EF	VF
	50·00	25·00

T12 10s.   Red on white (shades)
Prefix coding:
   Type 1: Letter over number and five digits.
   Type 2: Letter and figure "1" over number and five digits
   Type 3: Letter and figure "2" over number and five digits.
Quantity printed: Not known.
Serial letters:
   A to M

T13 10s.   Red on white (shades)   50·00   25·00
Prefix coding:
   Type 1: Letter over number and six digits.
   Type 2: Letter and figure "1" over number and six digits.
   Type 3: Letter and figure "2" over number and six digits.

T13 Type 1

Quantity printed: Not known.
Serial letters:
N to Z

Proof in black of T12/13

A most interesting proof (in black) of
T12/T13 is illustrated.

THE DARDANELLES CAMPAIGN OVERPRINTS

Despite extensive research little of substance has been found relating to
these rare and fascinating notes, apart from an official Treasury minute in
the Public Records Office, which states that £1 and 10s. currency notes
were issued for the use of the entire British Military Expeditionary Forces
in the Mediterranean and the Naval Expeditionary Forces in May–June
1915. Supplies of notes were apparently sent to Malta and Alexandria, but
those sent to Malta do not seem to have been overprinted: According to
the Inland Revenue log the notes were overprinted on 21 May 1915. The
translation of the T14 overprint reads: "Piastres silver 120" on the top line
and "Piastres silver one hundred and twenty" on the bottom. The T15
overprint reads: "Piastres silver 60" and "Piastres silver sixty".

A good article, entitled "Research on the Gallipoli Notes" by Fred
Philipson, will be found in the *International Bank Note Society Magazine,*
Vol. 10, No. 4, June 1971.

			Price	
			EF	VF
T14 £1	Black on white (red overprint)		from £1000	from £750

Prefix coding: Letter over number.
Quantity overprinted: Not known.
Serial letters:
F and J (and possibly others)

BRADBURY (*contd.*)

T14

T15

Sheet of T15

	EF	VF

T15 10s.   Red on white (black overprint)   £150   70·00
Prefix coding: Letter over number.
Quantity overprinted: Not known.
Serial letters:
Y and Z.

Third Issue

1917 (22 January) ONE POUND
Designed by Bertram Mackennal. Vignette of St. George and the Dragon based on the work of Benedetto Pistrucci for the Royal Mint. Photogravure-printed in sheets of 21 (3 × 7) by Waterlow Bros. and Layton on banknote paper manufactured by William Joynson and Co. with multiple watermark of Vandyck (diagonal) lines incorporating the Royal Cypher, the denomination ONE POUND and the four British emblems. Third-issue Treasury £1 notes measure 151 × 84 mm ($5\frac{15}{16}$ × $3\frac{5}{16}$ in.) and were legal tender until 1 August 1933.

		Price	
		EF	VF

T16 £1   Brown, purple and green (shades) on white
or cream
Prefix coding: Letter over number.
Quantity printed: 825 million.
Serial letters:

		EF	VF
A		22·00	10·00
B, C, D, E, F, G, H	each	20·00	8·00
Z		22·00	10·00

T16 showing dot

BRADBURY (*contd.*)

Common reverse of Third and Fourth Issue £1

Bradbury and Fisher £1 notes carrying the serial "Z" are from the bottom right-hand corner of the sheet, giving a ratio of 20 to 1. It is thought that these "Z" notes may have been used for control purposes.

1918 (22 October) TEN SHILLINGS
Designed by Bertram Mackennal. Photogravure-printed in sheets of 20 (4 × 5) by Waterlow Bros. and Layton on banknote paper manufactured by William Joynson and Co. with composite watermark incorporating the Royal Cypher, the denomination TEN SHILLINGS at the top and the four British emblems. Third-issue 10s. notes measures 138 × 78 mm ($5\frac{7}{16} \times 3\frac{1}{16}$ in.) and were legal tender until 1 August 1933. The serial number printed in BLACK.

		Price	
		EF	VF
T17 10s.	Green, purple and brown on white *Prefix coding:* Letter over number ("dot"). *Quantity printed:* 100 million. *Serial letter:*		
	A	60·00	25·00
T18 10s.	Green, purple and brown on white *Prefix coding:* Letter over number ("dash"). *Quantity printed:* Included in T17 above. *Serial letter:*		
	As in T17 above.	60·00	25·00

T18 showing dash

Common reverse of Third and Fourth Issue 10s.

1918 (16 December) TEN SHILLINGS
As last issue, but serial number is printed in RED.

<table>
<tr><td></td><td></td><td>Price</td><td></td></tr>
<tr><td></td><td>EF</td><td>VF</td></tr>
</table>

T19 10s.   Green, purple and brown on white
Prefix coding: Letter over number ("dot").
Quantity printed: 120 million.
Serial letters:
     B, C   *each* 50·00   20·00

T20 10s.   Green, purple and brown on white
Prefix coding: Letter over
number ("dash").
Quantity printed: included in
T19 above.
Serial letters:
     As in T19 above.   50·00   25·00

BRADBURY (*contd.*)

T21 proof

1917 (1 December) FIVE SHILLINGS
Ratified (i.e. approved for distribution) 21 February 1918. Designed by
Bertram Mackennal. Photogravure printed in sheets of 35 (5 × 7) by
Waterlow Bros. and Layton on banknote paper manufactured by
William Joynson and Co. with composite watermark incorporating the
Royal Cypher and the denomination FIVE SHILLINGS. Treasury 5s. notes,
signed by John Bradbury, measure 127 × 76 mm (5 × 3 in.) and were dis-
tributed to the clearing banks in Great Britain and Ireland, but were not
issued to the public. The notes were destroyed in November 1919.

		Price
		VF
T21 5s.	Deep violet and green on white	from £1000

                Prefix coding: Not known.
                Quantity printed: 7·9 million.
                Serial letters:
                Not known.

1918 (November) HALF-CROWN
Designed by C. Howard with vignette of King George V by T. S.
Harrison. Although proofs were prepared by De La Rue and Co., there
was no production run of Treasury 2s. 6d. notes signed by John Bradbury.

		Price	
		EF	*VF*
T22 2s. 6d.	Olive-green and chocolate on white	–	–

                Prefix coding: Not known.
                Quantity printed: None.
                Serial letters:
                Not allocated.

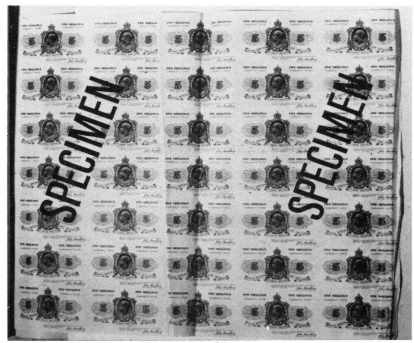

Sheet of T21

1918 (November) ONE SHILLING
   Designed by C. Howard with vignette of King George V by T. S.
   Harrison. Although proofs were prepared by De La Rue and Co., there
   was no production run of Treasury 1s. notes signed by John Bradbury.

T23 1s.   Green and brown on white   —   —
             Prefix coding: Not known.
             Quantity printed: None.
             Serial letters:
                 Not allocated.

2. Sir (Norman Fenwick) Warren Fisher (1879–1948)

Entered the Civil Service in 1903 and was posted to Inland Revenue
department, where he became private secretary to the Chairman of the
Board, Robert Chalmers, in 1907. After moving for a short time to the
National Health Insurance Commission for England in 1912, he returned
the following year to Somerset House as a Commissioner of Inland

FISHER (*contd.*)

Revenue. He was appointed Deputy Chairman of the Board in October 1914 and Chairman in August 1918. On 1 October 1919 Warren Fisher went to the Treasury as Permanent Secretary where he stayed until his retirement in 1939. He received a knighthood in 1919. Treasury notes signed by Fisher were of the same design as those of the Third Issue signed by Bradbury.

1919 (30 September) ONE POUND

Design, watermark and dimensions as Bradbury T16 above. Photogravure-printed in sheets of 21 (3 × 7) by Waterlow Bros. and Layton on banknote paper manufactured by William Joynson and Co.

		Price	
		EF	VF
T24 £1	Brown and green (shades) on white or cream		
	Prefix coding: Letter over number.		
	Quantity printed: 1250 million.		
	Serial letters:		
	K, L, M, N, O, P, R, S, T, U, W, X, Y *each*	18·00	7·00
	Z	20·00	8·00

For notes carrying the serial "Z" *see* under T16 and illustrated sheet.

1919 (30 September) TEN SHILLINGS

Design, watermark and dimensions as Bradbury T19 above. Photogravure-printed in sheets of 20 (4 × 5) by Waterlow Bros. and Layton on banknote paper manufactured by William Joynson and Co.

T25 10s.   Green, purple and brown on white
                Prefix coding: Letter over number ("dot").

T24

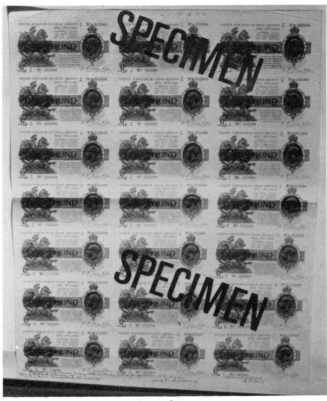

Sheet of T24

T26

FISHER (contd.)

    Quantity printed: 500 million.
Serial letters:
D, E, F, G, H   *each* 35·00   12·00

T26 10s. Green, purple and brown on white
Prefix coding: Letter over number ("dash").
Quantity printed: Included in T25 above.
Serial letters:
    As T25 above.   35·00   12·00

1919 (28 November) FIVE SHILLINGS
Design, watermark and dimensions as Bradbury T21 above.
Photogravure-printed in sheets of 35 (5 × 7) by Waterlow Bros. and
Layton on banknote paper manufactured by William Joynson and Co.
Although Treasury 5s. notes signed by Fisher were not officially issued a
few found their way into circulation.

T27

Price
VF

T27 5s. Violet and green on white
Prefix coding: Letter over number
Quantity printed: 10 million.
Serial letter:
    B   *from* £750

1919 (19 November) HALF-CROWN
Designed by C. Howard with vignette of King George V by T. S.
Harrison. Surface-printed in sheets of 40 (4 × 10) by De La Rue and Co.
on banknote paper manufactured by William Joynson and Co. with
composite watermark incorporating the Royal Cypher and the

Reverse of T27 common to Bradbury and Fisher

denomination HALF-CROWN. Treasury 2s. 6d. notes measure 117 × 75 mm
($4\frac{5}{8}$ × $2\frac{15}{16}$ in.) and were not officially issued. A few, however, found their
way into circulation.

Price
VF

T28 2s. 6d. Olive-green and chocolate on white
       Prefix coding: Letter over number.
       Quantity printed: 10 million.
       Serial letter:
    A   from £1000

T28

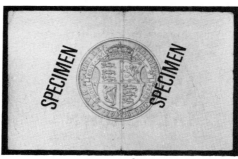

Reverse of T28

FISHER (*contd.*)

Sheet of T28

1919 (19 November) ONE SHILLING
Designed by C. Howard with vignette of King George V by T. S.
Harrison. Surface-printed in sheets of 49 (7 × 7) by De La Rue and Co.
on banknote paper manufactured by William Joynson and Co. with
composite watermark incorporating the Royal Cypher and the
denomination ONE SHILLING. Treasury 1s. notes measure 104 × 66 mm
(4⅛ × 2⅝ in.) and were not officially issued. A few, however, found their
way into circulation.

T29

Reverse of T29

Sheet of T29

FISHER (*contd.*)   *Price*
                                                          VF

T29 1s.   Green and brown on white
           Prefix coding: Letter over number.
           Quantity printed: 10 million.
           Serial letter:
                B   from £1000

1922 (6 November) TEN SHILLINGS
Design, watermark and dimensions as T25 above, but the word "No" is
omitted where it precedes the serial number. Photogravure-printed in
sheets of 20 (4 × 5) by Waterlow and Sons (who had taken over Waterlow
Bros. and Layton in 1920) on banknote paper manufactured by Portals
Ltd. (who replaced William Joynson).

                                                   Price
                                             EF   *VF*

T30 10s.   Green, purple and brown on white
           Prefix coding: Letter over number ("No"
           omitted)
           Quantity printed: 1100 million.
           Serial letters:
           J, K, L, M, N, O, P, R, S, T, U   *each* 25·00   8·00

T30

1923 (26 February) ONE POUND
Design and dimensions as T24 above, but watermark is now composite
so that the words ONE POUND appear in the top of each note.
Photogravure-printed in sheets of 21 (3 × 7) by Waterlow and Sons on
banknote paper manufactured by Portals Ltd.

T31 £1   Brown and green on white
           Prefix coding: Letter and figure "1" over
           number ("dot").

T31

		Price	
		EF	VF
Quantity printed: 2225 million.			
Serial letters:			
A1		18·00	6·00
B1, C1, D1, E1, F1, G1, H1, J1, K1, L1,			
M1, N1, O1, P1, R1, S1,			
T1, U1, W1, X1, Y1	*each*	16·00	4·00
Z1		18·00	6·00

For notes carrying the serial "Z" *see* under T16 and illustrated sheet.

			Price	
			EF	VF
T32	£1	Brown and green on white		
		Prefix coding: Letter and figure "1" over		
		number ("dash").		
		Quantity printed: Included in T31 above.		
		Serial letters:		
		As T31 above.	25·00	12·00

Since the dash, or to be more accurate, the square dot, appears on random notes in particular sheets, it may be found under any serial letter. Most examples, however, have turned up with H1 and M1 serials.

Fourth Issue

1927 (25 July) TEN SHILLINGS
Design, watermark and dimensions as T25 above, but following the

FISHER (*contd.*)

T33

passing of the Royal and Parliamentary Titles Act of 1927 into law, the wording on the notes was altered to read UNITED KINGDOM OF GREAT BRITAIN AND NORTHERN IRELAND. Photogravure-printed in sheets of 20 (4 × 5) by Waterlow and Sons.

T33 **10s.**   Green, purple and brown on white
                 Prefix coding: Letter over number ("No"
                 omitted).

Sheet of T33

Price

EF　　　VF

Quantity printed: 250 million.
Serial letters:
　T, U, W　　　　　　　　　　*each* 30·00　　10·00

T33 faulty watermark

FISHER (*contd.*)

T33 (faulty watermark)   Some of the notes of this issue have a faulty watermark. The fault, when it occurs, is on the fourth note of the
third row, i.e. notes with serial prefix numbers 12, 32, 52, 72
and 92. The fault is in a misshapen shamrock, which is not
properly indented on its right-hand side (*see* illustration).
Price (*VF*) £50

1927 (25 July) ONE POUND
Design, watermark and dimensions as T24 above, but wording is altered
to read UNITED KINGDOM OF GREAT BRITAIN AND NORTHERN IRELAND.
Photogravure-printed in sheets of 21 (3 × 7) by Waterlow and Sons.

T34

		Price	
		EF	VF

T34 £1   Brown and green on white
Prefix coding: Letter and figure "1" over
number ("dot").
Quantity printed: 550 million.
Serial letters:

		EF	VF
S1, T1, U1, W1, X1, Y1	*each*	25·00	8·00
Z1		27·00	10·00

For notes carrying the serial "Z" *see* under T16.

T35 £1   Brown and green on white
Prefix coding: Letter and figure "1" over
number ("dash").

| | Price | |
	EF	*VF*
Quantity printed: Included in T34 above		
Serial letters:		
As T34 above.	30·00	15·00

Since the dash, or to be more accurate, the square dot, appears on random notes in particular sheets, it may be found under any serial letter. Most examples, however, have turned up with S1 serials.

FROM THE BRADBURY THIRD ISSUE

The Bank of England and its Notes

Founded in 1694, the Bank of England is the pivot of British economy. It is the greatest banking institution ever created and today enjoys the trust and confidence that gave rise to the expression: "As safe as the Bank of England".

This was not always so. Indeed, when the Bank of England issued its first banknotes in 1694 they did not even have the status of legal tender. The Bank was forced to suspend payment on more than one occasion in its formative years and its very foundation has been described by some historians as an act of trickery.

Lord Macaulay, one of Britain's most able historians, wrote: "It was . . . not easy to guess that a Bill which purported only to impose a new duty on tonnage for the benefit of such persons as should advance money towards carrying on the war was really a Bill creating the greatest commercial institution that the world has ever seen."

During the reign of William and Mary (1689–1702) more money was needed to wage war with France. A Scotsman, William Paterson produced the idea which was drafted into a Bill "for granting to Their Majesties several Rates and Duties upon Tonnages of Ships and vessels and upon Beer, Ale and other Liquors; for securing certain Recompenses and Advantages in the said Act mentioned to such persons as shall voluntarily Advance the sum of Fifteen Hundred Thousand Pounds towards carrying on the War against France."

The promoters' "recompenses and advantages" were that they could raise £1,200,000 and create a Corporation to be named "The Governor and Company of the Bank of England". The capital was to be lent to the Government at 8% interest.

Evelyn's diary tells us "The first greate Bank for a fund of money being now established by Act of Parliament was fill'd and compleated to the sum of £120,000 [Evelyn was in error as the sum was £1,200,000] put under the government of the most able and wealthy citizens of London. All who ventur'd any sum had four per cent, so long as it lay in the Bank, and had power either to take it out at pleasure or transfer it."

Within two years of its foundation in 1694, the Bank of England was in trouble and had to suspend payments. The suspension of specie payments lasted from 13 July 1695 to 1697 and the notes depreciated to the extent that at one time they were being discounted at 17%. Accounts submitted to the House of Commons on 4 December 1696, indicated that £764,196 worth of notes were outstanding and were backed by only £35,664.

After the collapse of the South Sea Bubble the Bank was again in trouble in 1720, and a run on the Bank was successfully met by the somewhat farcical tactics of employing people to join the queues and withdraw money in large quantities of small change, taking it to the next window and redepositing. This slowed down the drain on the Bank's tills and allowed time for public alarm to subside.

When the Scottish Pretender was marching in the direction of London another crisis developed and the Bank of England used the same method to avert disaster.

By 1797 the Bank had enjoyed thirty years of successful banking and expansion, but other people had started banks and by 1793 there were about 400 note-issuing institutions in Britain. A combination of the war with France, the problems of the American colonists and the lack of regulation of note issues caused a general collapse of credit in that year. The situation worsened and although the Bank of England had "saved" a number of country banks, it was itself forced to suspend payments in 1797. From then until 1821 specie payment was suspended. It is worth noting that practically every bank in Europe suspended payments during the same period.

The next major crisis—in 1825—sowed the seeds for reform. The failure of Sir Peter Pole and Company led to 63 banks collapsing with consequences so severe that they were to be remembered bitterly for fifty years. The reserves of the Bank of England fell to £3,012,150 in November of that year.

Then, Sir Robert Peel introduced the Bank Charter Act of 1844 which severely restricted note issues of private banks and gave a monopoly to the Bank of England for issuing notes within a radius of sixty-five miles of London.

It was only in 1833 that by an Act of Parliament of William IV a limited legal-tender quality was given to Bank of England notes. Not until 1928 did the Bank of England £1 enjoy full legal-tender status.

The number of private banks issuing notes gradually decreased following Sir Robert Peel's Act and, in 1921, when Fox, Fowler and Co. of Wellington, Somerset, amalgamated with Lloyds Bank, the last English private banknotes ceased. The Isle of Man, however, issued private notes up to 1961.

Running Cash Notes

Running cash notes derive from the goldsmith notes which had been widely used by merchants from the reign of Charles I. The running cash note was a receipt for a deposit made out to bearer so that he could use it in a business transaction or present it to the Bank of England for payment in gold or silver.

The notes were entirely written by hand and, at first, were written on ordinary paper purchased from a stationers—a practice which soon ceased because of forgery. These notes could be part-paid. The holder could draw £5 from a note issued for £10 and have it duly recorded on the note, retaining the note as his receipt for the remaining £5 deposited in the Bank of England.

At first running cash notes were issued for odd amounts but before long they were made out for regular amounts.

1694   *Price*

B1   Hand-written amounts   −

Sealed Bills

These were not banknotes in the strict sense as they were promissory notes, normally bearing interest, issued against deposits or pledged assets. If they were intended to circulate from hand to hand they were unsuccessful and within twenty years went out of use altogether.

1694

B2   Hand-written amounts   −

Accomptable Notes

Introduced four days after the running cash notes, these were certificates of deposit and were not intended to serve as banknotes. They gave the depositor the right to "draw notes" on the Bank of England. Such withdrawals were then endorsed on the accomptable note. At a later date special forms were prepared by the Bank of England with a "check" pattern. The drawn notes were written by depositors on these forms which thus became an early version of the modern cheque.

It is interesting to note that the sealed bills, running cash notes and accomptable notes were all introduced in the first week of the Bank of England's existence. The first meeting of the Court of Directors of the Bank of England on 27 July 1694 was concerned with the ". . . method of giving Receipts for running cash . . .". The first decision was that "running cash notes" should be issued.

1694

B3   Hand-written amounts   −

Part-printed Notes

The first partially printed notes of the Bank of England have a Britannia medallion, possibly the work of John Sturt. The earliest known part-printed notes are those signed by Thomas Madockes, Chief Cashier from 1699 to 1739. For most of this time the Bank of England notes only circulated within a 20 mile radius of London.

Circa 1696
   Medallion of Britannia seated and holding spear and olive branch in top left-hand corner.

Price
B4   Hand-written amounts   –

1707
   Foliate border round Britannia medallion.
B5   Hand-written amounts   –

Part-printed Denominations

By 1745 notes were all printed in denominations of "round" figures. The word "pounds" was not printed so that an odd amount could still be written in on the note by hand if so required. The Bank of England possess one note for £28 10s. on which the words "eight pounds ten shillings" have been written in after the printed "Twenty".

1725–45
   Henry Portal paper. Printed by copper-plate.
B6   £20   Black on white (issued 1725)   –
B7   £30   Black on white   –
B8   £40   Black on white   –
B9   £50   Black on white   –
B10   £60   Black on white   –
B11   £70   Black on white   –
B12   £80   Black on white   –
B13   £90   Black on white   –
B14   £100   Black on white   –
B15   £200   Black on white   –
B16   £300   Black on white   –
B17   £400   Black on white   –
B18   £500   Black on white   –
B19   £1000   Black on white   –

Printed Denomination Notes (complete)

1759
Henry Portal paper. Copper-plate printing. The word "pound" or "pounds" printed after the amount.

B20	£10	Black on white (1759)	–
B21	£15	Black on white (1759)	–
B22	£25	Black on white (1765)	–

This practice was not adopted for other denomination notes until nearly the end of the eighteenth century.

Chief Cashier (Payee) Bank of England Notes

1. Abraham Newland (1782–1807)

1782
From 1752 the handwritten name of the payee was usually that of the Chief Cashier but from 1782 the Chief Cashier's name was used exclusively until 1855 when notes were made payable simply "to bearer".

			Price VF
B23	£10	Black on white	£600
B24	£15	Black on white	£600
B25	£20	Black on white	£600
B26	£25	Black on white	£600
B27	£30	Black on white	£800
B28	£40	Black on white	£1000
B29	£50	Black on white	£1200
B30	£60	Black on white (withdrawn 1803)	£4000
B31	£70	Black on white (withdrawn 1803)	£4800
B32	£80	Black on white (withdrawn 1803)	£6000
B33	£90	Black on white (withdrawn 1803)	£7200
B34	£100	Black on white	£1200
B35	£200	Black on white	£2000
B36	£300	Black on white	£4000
B37	£400	Black on white (withdrawn 1803)	£6000
B38	£500	Black on white	£5200
B39	£1000	Black on white	–

1793–97

The economic difficulties caused by the War with France made smaller denominations necessary. *Price VF*

B40	£1	Black on white (issued 1797)	£600
B41	£2	Black on white (issued 1797)	£1000
B42	£5	Black on white (issued 1793)	£600

Note—The famous Bank of England £1 note was first issued on 2 March 1797. Withdrawn in 1821 (except for an emergency issue 1825–26) it was not re-introduced until 1928.

1798

From this date the Chief Cashier's name was printed on the notes as payee.

B43	£1	Black on white	£600
B44	£2	Black on white	£1000
B45	£5	Black on white	£600
B46	£10	Black on white	£600
B47	£15	Black on white	£600
B48	£20	Black on white	£600
B49	£25	Black on white	£800
B50	£30	Black on white	£1200
B51	£40	Black on white	£2000
B52	£50	Black on white	£2000
B53	£100	Black on white	£1600
B54	£200	Black on white	£2000
B55	£300	Black on white	£4000
B56	£500	Black on white	£6000
B57	£1000	Black on white	–

1801 (31 July)

Year of issue on right side of note only.

B58	£1	Black on white	£600

2. Henry Hase (1807–29)

1807

Printed name of Chief Cashier as payee.

B59	£1	Black on white (countersigned)	£600
B60	£1	Black on white (un-countersigned)	£600
B61	£2	Black on white	£800
B62	£5	Black on white	£600
B63	£10	Black on white	£600
B64	£15	Black on white	£1200
B65	£20	Black on white	£640

HASE (contd.)

B76

			Price VF
B66	£25	Black on white	£2000
B67	£30	Black on white	£2000
B68	£40	Black on white	£2000
B69	£50	Black on white	£1600
B70	£100	Black on white	£1600
B71	£200	Black on white	£2000
B72	£300	Black on white	£4000
B73	£500	Black on white	£6000
B74	£1000	Black on white	—

1809

Printed dates and serial numbers. From 1809 the only part of the note not printed was the signature.

B75	£1	Black on white (1809)	£500
B76	£1	Black on white (1810–21)	£400
B77	£1	Black on white (1825)	£350
B78	£1	Black on white (1826)	£350
B79	£2	Black on white (1809	£800
B80	£5	Black on white	£600
B81	£10	Black on white	£600
B82	£15	Black on white (withdrawn 1822)	£1200
B83	£20	Black on white	£640
B84	£25	Black on white (withdrawn 1822)	£2800
B85	£30	Black on white	£2000

B77

			Price VF
B86	£40	Black on white	£2000
B87	£50	Black on white	£1600
B88	£100	Black on white	£1600
B89	£200	Black on white	£2000
B90	£300	Black on white	£4000
B91	£500	Black on white	£6000
B92	£1000	Black on white	–

Note—Nos. B77 and B78 were re-issues of the 1821 notes and can be identified by the date at the top reading "1821" while that across the centre reads: "1825 Decr. 20 London 20 Decr. 1825". It was an emergency issue.

Henry Hase Branch notes were issued from:
Gloucester (opened 19 July 1826)   Leeds (opened 1827)
Manchester (opened 21 Sept. 1826)   Exeter (opened 1827)
Swansea (opened 23 Oct. 1826)   Bristol (opened 1827)
Birmingham (opened 1826)   Newcastle (opened 1828)
Liverpool (opened 1827)

BRANCH NOTES

Notes which have the name of the branch printed on the banknote were introduced for the first time during this period. In all cases they are worth from twice as much as the normal "London" issues.

---

3. Thomas Rippon (1829–35)

1829
    Printed name of Chief Cashier as payee.

			Price VF
B93	£5	Black on white	£600
B94	£10	Black on white	£600
B95	£20	Black on white	£640
B96	£30	Black on white	£2000
B97	£40	Black on white	£2000
B98	£50	Black on white	£2000
B99	£100	Black on white	£1600
B100	£200	Black on white	£2000
B101	£300	Black on white	£4000
B102	£500	Black on white	£6000
B103	£1000	Black on white	—

Thomas Rippon Branch notes were issued from:

Gloucester	Bristol
Manchester	Newcastle
Swansea	Hull (opened 1829)
Birmingham	Norwich (opened 1829)
Liverpool	Plymouth (opened 1834)
Leeds	Portsmouth (opened 1834)
Exeter (closed in 1834)	

4. Matthew Marshall (1835–64)

1835–53
    Printed name of Chief Cashier as payee.

B104	£5	Black on white	£400
B105	£10	Black on white	£400
B106	£20	Black on white	£520
B107	£30	Black on white (withdrawn 1852)	£3200
B108	£40	Black on white (withdrawn 1851)	£2400
B109	£50	Black on white	£800
B110	£100	Black on white	£1400
B111	£200	Black on white	£2000
B112	£300	Black on white	£4000
B113	£500	Black on white	£6000
B114	£1000	Black on white	—

1853
    Printed signatures. Banknotes were completely printed from 1853. The

Chief Cashier, Matthew Marshall, is payee and the bank staff who signed the notes are as listed below.

			Price VF
B115 £5	Black on white (J. Vautin)		£400
B116 £5	Black on white (H. Bock)		£400
B117 £5	Black on white (J. Ferraby)		£400
B118 £10	Black on white (J. Vautin)		£400
B119 £10	Black on white (H. Bock)		£400
B120 £10	Black on white (J. Ferraby)		£400
B121 £20	Black on white (J. Williams)		£480
B122 £50	Black on white (J. Williams)		£800
B123 £100	Black on white (J. Williams)		£1400
B124 £200	Black on white (J. Luson)		£2000
B125 £300	Black on white (J. Luson)		£4000
B126 £500	Black on white (J. Luson)		£6000
B127 £1000	Black on white (J. Luson)		–

Pay to Bearer Bank of England Notes

1. Matthew Marshall (1835–64)

1855

The name of the Chief Cashier as payee is no longer used and the words "I Promise to pay the Bearer on Demand" replace it. Watermark of Matthew Marshall's signature introduced into the paper.

B128 £5	Black on white (J. Vautin)		£360
B129 £5	Black on white (H. Bock)		£360
B130 £5	Black on white (J. Ferraby)		£360
B131 £10	Black on white (J. Vautin)		£360
B132 £10	Black on white (H. Bock)		£360
B133 £10	Black on white (J. Ferraby)		£360
B134 £20	Black on white (J. Williams)		£400
B135 £50	Black on white (J. Williams)		£800
B136 £100	Black on white (J. Williams)		£1400
B137 £200	Black on white (J. Luson)		£2000
B138 £300	Black on white (J. Luson)		£4000
B139 £500	Black on white (J. Luson)		£6000
B140 £1000	Black on white (J. Luson)		–

1860

Signatures different from previous issues.

B141 £5	Black on white (W. P. Gattie)		£360
B142 £10	Black on white (W. P. Gattie)		£360
B143 £20	Black on white (T. Kent)		£400

MARSHALL (contd.)

			Price VF
B144	£50	Black on white (T. Kent)	£800
B145	£100	Black on white (T. Kent)	£1200
B146	£200	Black on white (C. T. Whitmel)	£2000
B147	£300	Black on white (C. T. Whitmel)	£4000
B148	£500	Black on white (C. T. Whitmel)	£6000
B149	£1000	Black on white (C. T. Whitmel)	–

Matthew Marshall Branch notes were issued from:

Gloucester	Newcastle
Manchester	Hull
Swansea	Norwich (closed 1852)
Birmingham	Plymouth
Liverpool	Portsmouth
Leeds	Leicester (opened 1843)
Bristol	

2. William Miller (1864–66)

1864–66

B150	£5	Black on white (W. P. Gattie)	£360
B151	£10	Black on white (W. P. Gattie)	£360
B152	£20	Black on white (T. Kent)	£400
B153	£50	Black on white (T. Kent)	£800
B154	£100	Black on white (T. Kent)	£1200
B155	£200	Black on white (C. T. Whitmel)	£2000
B156	£300	Black on white C. T. Whitmel)	£4000
B157	£500	Black on white (C. T. Whitmel)	£6000
B158	£1000	Black on white (C. T. Whitmel)	–

William Miller Branch notes as for Matthew Marshall.

3. George Forbes (1866–73)

1866–70

Notes printed two to a sheet and cut, causing three deckle edges and one straight edge.

B159	£5	Black on white (Hy Dixon)	£360
B160	£10	Black on white (Hy Dixon)	£320
B161	£20	Black on white (T. Puzey)	£400
B162	£50	Black on white (T. Puzey)	£800
B163	£100	Black on white (T. Puzey)	£1400
B164	£200	Black on white (W. O. Wheeler)	£2000
B165	£300	Black on white (W. O. Wheeler)	£4000

B166	£500	Black on white (W. O. Wheeler)	£6000
B167	£1000	Black on white (W. O. Wheeler)	–

Chief Cashier Printed Signature Bank of England Notes

The printed signature of the Chief Cashier appears on all Bank of England notes from 1870 together with the words "Chief Cashier" printed under the name.

1. George Forbes (1866–73)

1870

B168	£5	Black on white	£320
B169	£10	Black on white	£280
B170	£20	Black on white	£320
B171	£50	Black on white	£600
B172	£100	Black on white	£1200
B173	£200	Black on white	£2000
B174	£300	Black on white	£4000
B175	£500	Black on white	£6000
B176	£1000	Black on white	—

George Forbes Branch notes were issued from:

Gloucester	Bristol
Manchester	Newcastle
Swansea	Hull
Birmingham	Plymouth
Liverpool	Portsmouth (closed 1914)
Leeds	Leicester (closed 1872)

2. F. May (1873–93)

1873–93

B177	£5	Black on white	£280
B178	£10	Black on white	£240
B179	£20	Black on white	£240
B180	£50	Black on white	£600
B181	£100	Black on white	£1200
B182	£200	Black on white	£2000
B183	£300	Black on white (withdrawn 1885)	£4000
B184	£500	Black on white	£6000
B185	£1000	Black on white	—

MAY (contd.)

Note—Plate numbers are found under the medallion on the left side of the notes.

F. May Branch notes as for George Forbes.

3. H. G. Bowen (1893–1902)

1893–1902			Price VF
B186 £5	Black on white		£125
B187 £10	Black on white		£200
B188 £20	Black on white		£275
B189 £50	Black on white		£600
B190 £100	Black on white		£1000
B191 £200	Black on white		£2000
B192 £500	Black on white		£6000
B193 £1000	Black on white		—

H. G. Bowen Branch notes as for George Forbes.

4. John Gordon Nairne (1902–18)

Entered Bank service 1880. Chief Cashier 1902, Comptroller 1918, Director 1925–31.

1902–1918			
B194 £5	Black on white		£125
B195 £10	Black on white		£175
B196 £20	Black on white		£275
B197 £50	Black on white		£600
B198 £100	Black on white		£850
B199 £200	Black on white		£2000
B200 £500	Black on white		£6000
B201 £1000	Black on white		—

John Nairne Branch notes as for George Forbes.

5. Ernest Musgrave Harvey (1918–25)

Entered Bank service 1885, Chief Cashier 1918, Comptroller 1925, Director 1928–29, Deputy Governor 1929–36. Was awarded C.B.E. 1917, K.B.E. 1920. Baronet 1933, Chevalier of the Legion of Honour 1918. Chevalier of the Order of Leopold of Belgium 1919.

B202

1918–25			Price VF
B202 £5	Black on white		£45
B203 £10	Black on white		£55
B204 £20	Black on white		£125
B205 £50	Black on white		£450
B206 £100	Black on white		£550
B207 £200	Black on white		£2000
B208 £500	Black on white		£6000
B209 £1000	Black on white		—

Ernest Harvey Branch notes as for George Forbes.

Modern Bank of England Notes (from 1928)

The Bank of England assumed the responsibility for the printing and issue of currency notes on 28 November 1928, under the Currency and Banknotes Act 1928, and in July 1933 the Treasury notes were withdrawn from circulation.

The Bank's first issue of Green (Britannia) £1 notes and red-brown 10s. notes were signed by the Chief Cashier, C. P. Mahon, and joined the existing high-denomination notes of £5 and above.

In 1940, following the outbreak of War, the colour of the £1 and 10s. notes was changed to blue and mauve respectively and a metal thread—the invention of Mr. S. B. Chamberlain, General Manager of the Bank's printing works—was inserted.

In 1943, following the appearance of German forgeries, it was decided to withdraw the denominations above £5. It was 20 years before the £10 note was to reappear and nearly 30 years before the country again had a £20 note.

Also during the War the Bank, fearing that there would be difficulties in transporting coinage, prepared small-denomination notes of 2s. 6d. and 5s. Although these were not needed and were destroyed after the War, a few specimens did in fact find their way into the hands of collectors.

In 1948 £1 and 10s. notes of the pre-war colours, green and red-brown, were again issued and for a short time were unthreaded to use up old stocks of paper. Subsequently all Bank of England notes carried the now familiar metal thread as a security precaution.

In 1956 white £5 notes were discontinued (they were withdrawn in 1961) and the following year, 1957, saw the issue of a new design of £5 by Stephen Gooden, featuring the helmeted head of Britannia on the obverse with a Lion and Key reverse.

The next major change was in the spring of 1960 when the Bank unveiled its new issue £1, designed by Robert Austin, and bearing for the first time a portrait of the Queen on the obverse. The 10s. followed 18 months later; then in 1963 came the £5 and in 1964 the £10—these last two designed by Reynolds Stone.

In 1970 a £20 note—the first in a new more imaginative series of pictorial designs by Harry Eccleston—made its appearance. In addition to the portrait of the Queen, the note carries on the obverse a vignette of St. George and the Dragon, and on the reverse a statue of Shakespeare and the balcony scene from Romeo and Juliet.

The £5 note, issued in November 1971, features the Duke of Wellington and a battle scene from the Peninsular War on the reverse, while the obverse carries the Queen's portrait alongside a vignette of Winged Victory and a medallion of Britannia.

The £10 note, issued in February 1975, features Florence Nightingale and a hospital scene from the Crimean War on the reverse, while the obverse carries the Queen's portrait in State Robes.

The Bank of England is expected to complete the series with a pictorial design for the £1 in 1977–78.

1. Cyril Patrick Mahon (1925–29)

Born 1882. Entered Bank service 1901. Chief Cashier 1 April 1925. Comptroller 1929–32.

On 22 November 1928 the Bank of England 10s. note was introduced for the first time and the £1 note was re-introduced after a gap of over 100 years. The new banknotes, signed by the Chief Cashier, C. P. Mahon, were designed collectively by various experts in art and printing, and showed on the obverse a medallion by Daniel Maclise of Britannia seated (originally used for high-denomination notes of the 1850s). The reverse of the £1 showed the Bank of England prior to re-building, above a machined pattern of blue, pale green and mauve, while the reverse of the 10s. had two value tablets blended into scroll patterns. The notes were plate-printed in sheets of 24 at St. Luke's Works, Old Street, London, on banknote paper manufactured by Portals Ltd, with a watermark of wavy lines and the helmeted head of Britannia facing right. BRITANNIA £1 notes—as they are usually known—measure 151 × 85 mm (6 × 3⅜ in.) and were legal tender until 28 May 1962. The 10s. notes measure 140 × 78 mm (3 1/16 × 5½ in.) and were legal tender until 29 October 1962.

		Price	
		EF	VF
B210 10s.	Red-brown		
	Prefix coding: Letter, number, number.		
	Width of design: 126 mm.		
	Quantity printed: 410 million.		
	Serial letters:		
	A01 (one million notes of inaugural run)	75·00	40·00
	Z— (first series traced from Z01)	35·00	15·00
	Y—, X—, W—	each 25·00	8·00
	V— (last series traced to V11)	35·00	12·00
B211 10s.	Red-brown replacement note	*	*
	Prefix coding: Not known.		
	Quantity printed: Not known.		
	Serial letters: Not yet traced.		
B212 £1	Green		
	Prefix coding: Letter, number, number.		

B210

MAHON (contd.)

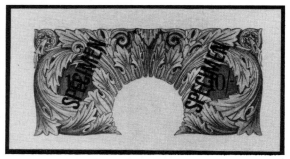

Common reverse to 10s.

Width of design (i.e. signature block):
Plate 1: 137·5 mm.
Plate 2: 138·5 mm.
Quantity printed: 725 million.
Serial letters:

	Price EF	VF
A01 (one million notes of inaugural run).	70·00	35·00
A— (first series traced from A16)	25·00	7·00
B—, C—, D—, E—, F—, G—	each 22·00	7·00
H— (last series traced to H30)	30·00	9·00

No price distinction between plates 1 and 2 notes.

B213 £1   Green replacement note   *   *
Prefix coding: Not known.
Quantity printed: Not known.
Serial letters: Not yet traced.

B212

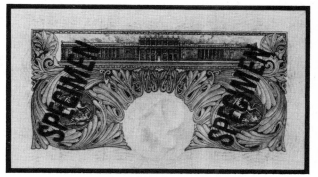

Common reverse to Britannia £1 from Mahon to O'Brien

B214 £1

B214 10s. with matching serial number

MAHON (*contd.*)

B214 envelope

B214   £1 and 10s. notes with matching serial numbers in presentation parchment envelope, inscribed "BANK OF ENGLAND 22 November 1928". 100 pairs only believed issued.   Price (EF) £350.

For classification of specimen notes and errors *see* page 102.

1925 (date unknown)

Large denomination notes from FIVE POUNDS to ONE THOUSAND POUNDS, bearing various dates between 1925 and 1929, were issued with the signature of C. P. Mahon. Of traditional design, lettering and watermark, these notes measured 212 × 135 mm (8⅜ × 5⁵⁄₁₆ in.) and were plate-printed in pairs (then cut, leaving one straight edge and three deckled) at St. Luke's Works, London, on banknote paper manufactured by Portals Ltd. Notes of £10 and above were legal tender until 1 May 1945, and £5 notes without metal thread until 1 March 1946.

			Price	
			EF	VF
B215	£5	Black on white	30·00	15·00
B216	£10	Black on white	45·00	20·00
B217	£20	Black on white	75·00	40·00
B218	£50	Black on white	From £200	

B215

		EF
B219 £100	Black on white	From £350
B220 £200	Black on white (discontinued 1928)	From £2000
B221 £500	Black on white	From £3000
B222 £1000	Black on white	From £4000

In addition to London, the Bank of England also issued large denomination notes drawn on various branches. These were:

Birmingham	Liverpool
Bristol	Manchester
Gloucester	Newcastle
Hull	Plymouth
Leeds	Swansea

Branch notes, when available, are priced from 15% above those from London.

---

2. Basil Gage Catterns (1929–34)

Born 1886. Entered Bank service 1908, Chief Cashier 1929, Director 1934–36 and 1945–48, Deputy Governor 1936–45.

CATTERNS (*contd.*)

B223

1930 (15 July) TEN SHILLINGS
Design, watermark and dimensions as for C. P. Mahon, but larger plates
used for some notes. Printed at St. Luke's Works, London.

		Price	
		EF	VF
B223 10s.	Red-brown		
	Prefix coding: Letter, number, number.		
	Width of design:		
	Plate 1: 126 mm.		
	Plate 2: 128 mm.		
	Quantity printed: 965 million.		
	Serial letters:		
	V— (first series traced from V14)	25·00	9.00
	U—, T—, S—, R—,		
	O—, N—, M—, L—	*each* 20.00	7.00
	K— (last series traced to K97)	22·00	8·00

For plate 2 notes add 20% to the above prices.

B224	Red-brown replacement note	*	*
	Prefix coding: Not known.		
	Quantity printed: Not known.		
	Serial letters: Not yet traced.		

1930 (15 July) ONE POUND
Design, watermark and dimensions as for C. P. Mahon, but larger plates
used for some notes. Printed at St. Luke's Works, London.

B225 £1   Green
Prefix coding: Letter, number, number.

	EF	VF

Width of design (*i.e. signature block*):
   Plate 1: 137·5 mm.
   Plate 2: 138·5 mm.
Quantity printed: 1450 million.
Serial letters:

	EF	VF
H— (first series traced from H33)	20·00	8·00
J—, K—, L—, M—,		
N—, O—, R—, S—,		
T—, U—, W—, X—,		
Y— each	15·00	6·00
Z— (last series traced to Z99)	17·00	6·50

No price distinction between plate 1 and plate 2 notes.

B226 £1   Green
Prefix coding: Number, number, letter
Width of design (*i.e., signature block*):
   138·5 mm.
Quantity printed: 99 million.
Serial letters:

	EF	VF
—A (series traced from 08A to 99A)	25·00	9·00
—B (series not yet traced)		

B227 £1   Green replacement note   *   *
Prefix coding: Not known.
Quantity printed: Not known.
Serial letters: Not yet traced.

For classification of specimen notes and errors *see* page 102.

1929 (date unknown)

Large denomination notes from FIVE POUNDS to ONE THOUSAND POUNDS,
bearing various dates between 1929 and 1934. Design, watermark and

B225

CATTERNS (*contd.*)

B229

dimensions as for C. P. Mahon notes. Printed at St. Luke's Works, London.

B232 Bristol Branch note

			Price	
			EF	VF
B228	£5	Black on white	30·00	15·00
B229	£10	Black on white	45·00	20·00
B230	£20	Black on white	75·00	40·00
B231	£50	Black on white	From £200	
B232	£100	Black on white	From £350	
B233	£500	Black on white	From £3000	
B234	£1000	Black on white	From £4000	

Branch notes, when available, are priced from 15% above those from London. For full details *see* page 49.

---

3. Kenneth Oswald Peppiatt (1934–49)

Born 1893. Entered Bank service 1911. Chief Cashier 1934. Director 1949–57, K.B.E. 1941.

FIRST PERIOD (1934–39)

1934 (5 October) TEN SHILLINGS
Design, watermark and dimensions as for C. P. Mahon, but larger plates used for some notes. Printed at St. Luke's Works, London.

			Price	
			EF	VF
B235	10s.	Red-brown		
		Prefix coding: Letter, number, number.		
		Width of design:		
		Plate 1: 126 mm.		
		Plate 2: 128 mm.		
		Quantity printed: 128 million.		
		Serial letters:		
		J— (first series traced from J01)	18·00	5·00
		H—, E—, D—, C—, B—	each 16·00	3·50
		A— (last series traced to A99)	20·00	5·00

For plate 2 notes add 25% to the above prices.

B236	10s.	Red-brown		
		Prefix coding: Number, number, letter.		
		Width of design:		
		Plate 1: 126 mm.		
		Plate 2: 128 mm.		
		Quantity printed: 850 million.		

PEPPIATT (*contd.*)   *Price*

                                                      EF   *VF*

         Serial letters:

            —Z (first series traced from 01Z)   14·00   4·00

            —Y, —X, —W, —U, —T, —S, —R *each*   12·00   3·50

            —O (last series traced to O32)   14·00   4·00

No examples have been found of serial letters —N and —M which were probably destroyed in the blitz in 1940. For plate 2 notes add 10% to the above prices.

B237 10s.   Red-brown replacement note   *   *

            Prefix coding: Not known.

            Quantity printed: Not known.

            Serial letters: Not yet traced.

B235

B236

B238

1934 (17 October) ONE POUND
Design, watermark and dimensions as for C. P. Mahon notes. Printed at
St. Luke's Works, London.

	Price	
	EF	VF

B238 £1   Green
Prefix coding: Number, number, letter.
Width of design–signature block: 138·5 mm
Quantity printed: 1880 million.
Serial letters:

	EF	VF
—B (first series traced from 17B)	12·00	4·00
—C, —D, —E, —H, —J, —K, —L,		
—M, —N, —O, —R,		
—S, —T, —U, —W,		
—X, —Y	*each* 10·00	3·00
—Z (last series traced to 99Z)	10·00	4·00

B239 £1   Green
Prefix coding: Letter, number, number,
letter.
Width of design (i.e. signature block):
138·5 mm.
Quantity printed: 850 million.
Serial letters:

	EF	VF
A—A (first series traced from A10A)	12·00	4·00
B—A, C—A, D—A, E—A, H—A,		
J—A, K—A,	*each* 10·00	3·00
L—A (last series traced to L35A)	11·00	3·50

No examples have been found of serial letters M—A, N—A and O—A,
which were probably destroyed in the blitz of 1940.

PEPPIATT (contd.)

B239

	Price	
	EF	*VF*
B240 £1 Green replacement note	*	*

Prefix coding: Not known.
Quantity printed: Not known.
Serial letters: Not yet traced.

For classification of specimen notes and errors *see* page 102.

1934 (August)

Large denomination notes from FIVE POUNDS to ONE THOUSAND POUNDS, bearing various dates between August 1934 and August 1943. Design, watermark and dimensions as for C. P. Mahon notes. Printed at St. Luke's Works, London.

B241	£5	Black on white	25·00	15·00
B242	£10	Black on white	45·00	20·00
B243	£20	Black on white	75·00	40·00
B244	£50	Black on white	From £200	
B245	£100	Black on white	From £350	
B246	£500	Black on white	From £3000	
B247	£1000	Black on white	From £4000	

Branch notes, when available, are priced from 15% above those for London. For full details *see* page 49. Branch notes were discontinued on the outbreak of War in 1939.

B247

SECOND PERIOD (1940–48)

1940 (29 March) ONE POUND
The blue emergency issue incorporating a metal thread—the invention of the General Manager of the Bank's printing works, Mr. S. B. Chamberlain. Basic design and dimensions unchanged, but a double line now surrounded the unprinted part on the front containing the Britannia watermark. Plate-printed ("A" series only) until September 1940 at St. Luke's Works, London, on banknote paper manufactured by Portals Ltd. Thereafter by offset-litho at Overton, Hampshire. Emergency issue £1 notes were legal tender until 28 May 1962.

		Price	
		EF	*VF*
B248 £1	Pale blue (shades): "A" series		
	Prefix coding: Letter, number, number, letter.		
	Quantity printed: 297 million.		
	Width of design (i.e. signature block): 140 mm.		
	Serial letters:		
	A—D (series traced from A01D)	12·00	4·00
	A—E (series traced from A05E)	7·50	2·50
	A—H (series traced from A04H)	7·50	2·50

PEPPIATT (contd.)

B249

	Price	
	EF	*VF*

B249 £1   Blue (shades)
Prefix coding: Letter, number, number,
letter.
Width of design (i.e. signature block):
140–142 mm.
Quantity printed: 5148 million.
Serial letters:

    B—D, C—D, D—D, E—D, H—D,
    J—D, K—D, L—D, M—D, N—D,
    O—D, R—D, S—D, T—D, U—D,

W—D, X—D, Y—D	*each* 4·50	2·00
Z—D (last series traced to Z74D)	6·00	3·00

    B—E, C—E, D—E, E—E, H—E,
    J—E, K—E, L—E, M—E, N—E,
    O—E, R—E, S—E, T—E, U—E,

W—E	*each* 4·50	2·00

    X—E (series not yet traced)
    Y—E (series not yet traced)
    Z—E (series not yet traced)

    B—H, C—H, D—H, E—H, H—H,
    J—H, K—H, L—H, M—H, N—H,
    O—H, R—H, S—H, T—H, U—H,

W—H, X—H	*each* 4·50	2·00

    Y—H (series not yet traced)
    Z—H (series not yet traced)

B250 £1   Blue replacement note
            Prefix coding: Not known.
            Quantity printed: Not known.
            Serial letters: Not yet traced.

1940 (2 April) TEN SHILLINGS
The mauve emergency issue, incorporating a metal thread as the £1
above. Basic design and dimensions unchanged. Plate-printed until
September 1940 at St. Luke's Works, London, on banknote paper
manufactured by Portals Ltd. Thereafter by offset-litho at Overton,
Hampshire. Emergency issue 10s. notes were legal tender until 29 October 1962.

		Price	
		EF	VF
B251 10s.	Mauve (shades)		
	Prefix coding: Letter, number, number, letter.		
	Width of design: 129 mm.		
	Quantity printed: 2200 million.		
	Serial letters:		
	Z—D (first series traced from Z02D)	7·50	2·50
	Y—D, X—D, W—D, U—D, T—D,		
	S—D, R—D, O—D, N—D, M—D,		
	L—D, K—D, J—D, H—D, E—D,		
	D—D, C—D, B—D	*each* 6·00	2·00
	A—D (last series traced to A98D)	7·50	2·50
	Z—E (first series traced from Z02E)	7·50	2·00
	Y—E	6·00	2·00
	X—E (last series traced to X15E)	7·50	2·00

B251

PEPPIATT (contd.)

B252 10s.   Mauve replacement note   *   *
Prefix coding: Not known.
Quantity printed: Not known.
Serial letters: Not yet traced.
For classification of specimen notes and errors *see* page 102.

1941 (date unknown)
The emergency small-denomination notes of FIVE SHILLINGS and HALF-CROWN (signed K. O. Peppiatt) were prepared by the Bank of England on instructions from H.M. Government, who feared there might be difficulties in transporting coinage. The notes, which were printed on un-watermarked paper with the design on both sides, incorporate a metal thread, and measure 114 × 73 mm (4½ × 2⅞ in.). Although they were distributed to the clearing banks, the notes were never issued to the public and were destroyed in the late 1940s. Examples which have survived have no serial numbers.

B253

B254

Price
VF

B253 5s.   Olive-green (design) on pale pink (background) From £750
Prefix coding: None.
Widths of design and signature block: 98 mm
and 104 mm.
Quantity printed: Not known.
Serial letters: None.

B254 2s. 6d. Black (design) on pale blue (background)   From £750
Prefix coding: None.
Widths of design and signature block:
105 mm and 103 mm.
Quantity printed: Not known.
Serial letters: None.

1945 (18 October) FIVE POUNDS
Design, watermark and dimensions as for C. P. Mahon notes, but metal thread is now incorporated and all four edges are straight. The notes, which were printed at St. Luke's Works, London, were legal tender until 13 March 1961. (Although the notes were not issued until 1945, many of them bear dates from 1944 on.)

			Price	
			EF	*VF*
B255 £5	Black on white			

Prefix coding: Letter, number, number.
Quantity printed: 397 thousand.
Serial letters:

		EF	VF
E— (first series traced from E01 dated			
2 September 1944)		20·00	12·00
H—, J—, K—	*each*	20·00	12·00

THIRD PERIOD (1948)

1948 (17 June)
Re-issue of the unthreaded pre-war TEN SHILLINGS and ONE POUND notes. This enabled the Bank of England to use up stockpiled notes and supplies of paper without the metal thread. The design, dimensions and watermark were the same as for C. P. Mahon, but in the case of the £1 larger plates were used. The notes were printed at St. Luke's Works, London.

PEPPIATT (*contd.*)

B256

		Price	
		EF	VF

B256 10s. Red-brown
Prefix coding: Number, number, letter.
Width of design:
  Plate 1: 126 mm.
  Plate 2: 129 mm.
Quantity printed: 75 million.
Serial letter:
  —L (series traced from 10L to 70L)   15·00   8·00

B257 10s. Red-brown replacement note   *   *
Prefix coding: Not known.
Quantity printed: Not known.
Serial letter: Not yet traced.

B258

		EF	*VF*

B258 £1   Green
Prefix coding: Letter, number, number, letter.
Width of design (i.e. signature block): 141·5 mm.
Quantity printed: 135 million.
Serial Letters:

	EF	*VF*
R—A (first traced from R01A)	12·00	5·00
S—A (last series traced to S35A)	15·00	5·00

B259 £1   Green replacement note
Prefix coding: Letter, number, number, letter.
Quantity printed: Not known.
Serial letters: Not yet traced.

For classification of specimen notes and errors, *see* page 102.

FOURTH PERIOD (1948–49)

1948 (13 September) ONE POUND
Design, watermark and dimensions as for C. P. Mahon, but metal thread is now incorporated and larger plates are used. Printed at St. Luke's Works, London.

B260 £1   Green
Prefix coding: Letter, number, number, letter.
Width of design (i.e. signature block):
    Plate 1: 141·5 mm.
    Plate 2: 143·5 mm.
    Plate 3: 145 mm.

B260

PEPPIATT (contd.)

Price

		EF	VF
Quantity printed: 1190 million.			
Serial letters:			
S—A (first series traced from S41A)		12·00	4·00
T—A, U—A, W—A, X—A, Y—A	each	7·00	3·00
Z—A (last series traced to Z99A)		9·00	3·50
A—B (first series traced from A34B)		8·00	3·00
B—B, C—B, D—B, E—B	each	7·00	3·00
H—B (last series traced to H36B)		11·00	4·00

For plate 2 and plate 3 notes add 20% to the above prices.

B261 £1   Green replacement note
Prefix coding: Letter, number, number, letter.
Quantity printed: 9 million.
Serial letters:
S—S (series traced from S01S to S09S) 35·00 15·00

1948 (25 October) TEN SHILLINGS
Design, watermark and dimensions as for C. P. Mahon, but metal thread is now incorporated and larger plates are used for some notes. Printed at St. Luke's Works, London.

B262 10s.   Red-brown
Prefix coding: Number, number, letter.
Width of design:
Plate 1: 126 mm.
Plate 2: 129 mm.
Plate 3: 131 mm.
Quantity printed: 420 million.

B262

	Price	
	EF	VF

Serial letters:

—L (first series traced from 73L)   20·00   12·00

—K, —J, —H   *each* 12·00   4·00

—E (last series traced to 90E)   12·00   4·00

—D (series not yet traced)

For plate 1 notes add 25% to the above prices. For plate 3 notes add 50% to the above prices.

B263   10s.   Red-brown replacement note
Prefix coding: Number, number, letter.
Quantity printed: 6 million (estimated)
Serial letter:

—A (series traced from 01A to 03A)   50·00   25·00

1948 (9 September) FIVE POUNDS
Design, watermark and dimensions as for K. O. Peppiatt notes of Second Period (B255), but thin paper is used, and all notes are dated 1947. Printed at St. Luke's Works, London.

B264   £5   Black on white
Prefix coding: Letter, number, number.
Quantity printed: 198 thousand.
Serial letters:

L—, M—   25·00   12·00

For classification of specimen notes and errors *see* page 102.

B264

PEPPIATT (*contd.*)

SUMMARY OF MAIN TYPES OF PEPPIATT NOTES

Confusion has arisen over the identification of the four main types of Peppiatt notes. They are:

TEN SHILLINGS: Type 1   Pre-war Letter, number, number (unthreaded)
                Type 2*a* Pre-war Number, number, letter (unthreaded)
                    2*b* Post-war Number, number, letter (unthreaded)
                Type 3   Wartime Letter, number, number, letter (threaded)
                Type 4   Post-war Number, number, letter (threaded)

ONE POUND: Type 1   Pre-war Number, number, letter (unthreaded)
                Type 2*a* Pre-war Letter, number, number, letter (unthreaded)
                    2*b* Post-war Letter, number, number, letter (unthreaded)
                Type 3   Wartime Letter, number, number, letter (threaded)
                Type 4   Post-war Letter, number, number, letter (threaded)

Some notes on shading. St. Luke's Works, London was hit by two bombs on the night of 9/10 September 1940 and production of banknotes was then transferred to emergency premises near the Bank's paper suppliers, Portals, in Hampshire. Up to the move printing had been completed of the "A" serial £1 notes only. Although these notes have previously been distinguished by their pale blue colour, the same shades can be found in later issues. Students of shading may clearly identify at least 20 combinations of colours of colour based on the following colour breakdown:

Obverse main design	*Obverse background*
Pale blue	Pink
Blue	Deep pink
Deep blue (ultramarine)	Buff

Obverse signature block	*Reverse*
Light shading	Pale blue
Medium shading	Blue
Heavy shading	Greenish-blue

> ### 4. Percival Spencer Beale (1949–55)

Born 1906. Entered Bank service 1924. Chief Cashier 1949.

1950 (17 March) TEN SHILLINGS
Design, watermark and dimensions as for K. O. Peppiatt notes of the
Fourth Period. Printed at St Luke's Works, London.

		Price	
		EF	VF
B265 10s.	Red-brown		
	Prefix coding: Number, number, letter.		
	Width of design: 129 mm.		
	Quantity printed: 300 million.		
	Serial letters:		
	—E (series not yet traced)		
	—D (first series traced from 04D)	9·00	4·00
	—C, —B (last series traced to 94B)	*each* 8·00	4·00

B265

B266 10s.	Red-brown		
	Prefix coding: Letter, number, number, letter.		
	Width of design: 129 mm.		
	Quantity printed: 1668 million.		
	Serial letters:		
	Z—Z (first series traced from Z19Z)	8·50	3·00
	Y—Z, X—Z, W—Z, U—Z, T—Z, S—Z, R—Z, O—Z, N—Z, M—Z, L—Z, K—Z, J—Z, H—Z, E—Z	*each* 5·50	2·50
	D—Z (last series traced to D85Z)	8·50	3·00

BEALE (*contd.*)

B266

		Price	
		EF	*VF*

B267 10s.   Red-brown replacement note
Prefix coding: Number, number letter.
Quantity printed: 30 million.
Serial letter:
—A (series traced from 06A to 34A)   35·00   15·00

1950 (17 March) ONE POUND

Design, watermark and dimensions as for K. O. Peppiatt notes of the
Fourth Period. Printed at St. Luke's Works, London.

B268 £1   Green
Prefix coding: Letter, number, number,
   letter.
Width of design (i.e. signature block):
   141·5 mm.
Quantity printed: 4275 million.
Serial letters:
   H—B (first series traced from H38B)   9·00   3·50
   J—B, K—B, L—B, M—B, N—B,
   O—B, R—B, S—B, T—B, U—B,
   W—B, X—B, Y—B   *each* 4·50   2·00
   Z—B (last series traced to Z64B)   5·00   2·50

	Price	
	EF	*VF*
A—C (first series traced from A03C)	5·00	2·50
B—C, C—C, D—C, E—C, H—C,		
J—C, K—C, L—C, M—C, N—C,		
O—C, R—C, S—C, T—C, U—C,		
W—C, X—C, Y—C *each*	4·50	2·00
Z—C (last series traced to Z80C)	5·00	2·50
A—J (first series traced from A11J)	5·00	2·50
B—J, C—J, D—J, E—J, H—J, K—J *each*	4·50	2·00
L—J (last series traced to L63J)	9·00	3·50

B269 £1 Green replacement note
Prefix coding: Letter, number, number, letter.
Quantity printed: 60 million.
Serial letters:

S—S (series traced from S10S to S68S)	20·00	12·00

B269

1949 (13 December) FIVE POUNDS
Design, watermark and dimensions as for K. O. Peppiatt notes of the Second Period (B255). Printed at St. Luke's Works, London.

B270 £5 Black on white
Prefix coding: Letter, number, number.
Quantity printed: 892 thousand.

BEALE (contd.)

B270

Price

EF   VF

Serial letters:

N—, R—, S—, T—, U—, V—, W—,

X—, Y—   *each* 18·00   10·00

For classification of specimen notes and errors *see* page 102.

---

5. Leslie Kenneth O'Brien (1955–62)

Born 1908. Entered Bank service 1927. Chief Cashier 1955. Director 1962–64. Deputy Governor 1964–66. Governor 1966–73. First member of the bank's ordinary staff to become Governor. Knighted 1967 and became Lord O'Brien of Lothbury in 1973.

FIRST (Britannia) PERIOD (1955–60)

1955 (21 November) TEN SHILLINGS
Design, watermark and dimensions as for K. O. Peppiatt notes of the Fourth Period. Printed at St. Luke's Works, London.

B271

	Price	
	EF	VF

B271 10s.   Red-brown
Prefix coding: Letter, number, number, letter.
Width of design: 129 mm.
Quantity printed: 2500 million.
Serial letters:

D—Z (first series traced from D86Z)	9·00	4·00
C—Z, B—Z	4·00	2·00
A—Z (last series traced to A93Z)	6·00	2·50
Z—Y (first series traced from Z03Y)	5·00	2·50
Y—Y, X—Y, W—Y, U—Y, T—Y, S—Y, R—Y, O—Y, N—Y, M—Y, L—Y, K—Y, J—Y, H—Y, E—Y, D—Y, C—Y, B—Y *each*	4·00	2·00
A—Y (last series traced to A97Y)	5·00	2·50
Z—X (first series traced from Z04X)	5·00	2·50
Y—X (last series traced to Y15X)	5·00	2·50

B272

O'BRIEN (*contd.*)   Price

                                                        EF   VF

B272 10s.   Red-brown replacement note
            Prefix coding: Number, number, letter.
            Quantity printed: 35 million.
            Serial letter:
            —A (series traced from 36A to 67A)   30·00   15·00

1955 (21 November) ONE POUND
Design, watermark and dimensions as for K. O. Peppiatt notes of the
Fourth Period. Printed at St. Luke's Works, London.

                                                        Price
                                                   EF   VF

B273 £1   Green
           Prefix coding: Letter, number, number,
           letter.
           Width of design (*i.e. signature block*):
           141·5 mm.
           Quantity printed: 3900 million.
           Serial letters:
           L—J (first series traced from L65J)   8·00   3·50
           M—J, N—J, O—J, R—J, S—J, T—J,
           U—J, W—J, X—J, Y—J   *each* 4·00   2·00
           Z—J (last series traced to Z98J)   5·00   2·00
           A—K (first series traced from A22K)   5·00   2·00
           B—K, C—K, D—K, E—K, H—K,
           J—K, K—K, L—K, M—K, N—K,
           O—K, R—K, S—K, T—K, U—K,
           W—K, X—K, Y—K   *each* 4·00   2·00
           Z—K (last series traced to Z76K)   5·00   2·00

B273

		EF	VF
A—L (first series traced from A14L)		5·00	2·00
B—L, C—L, D—L, E—L, H—L,			
J—L	each	4·00	2·00
K—L (last series traced to K12L)		6·00	3·50

B274 £1   Green replacement note
Prefix coding:
Quantity printed: 55 million.
Serial letters:

	EF	VF
S—S (series traced from S73S to S99S)	30·00	12·00
S—T (series traced from S01T to S22T)	35·00	15·00

1955 (5 July) FIVE POUNDS
   Design, watermark and dimensions as for K. O. Peppiatt notes of the Second Period (B255). Printed at St. Luke's Works, London.

	Price	
	EF	VF

B275 £5   Black on white
Prefix coding: Letter, number, number.
Quantity printed: 99 thousand.
Serial letter:

	EF	VF
Z—	20·00	10·00

B276

O'BRIEN (contd.)

Price

EF   VF

B276 £5   Black on white
Prefix coding: Letter, number, number,
        letter.
Quantity printed: 375 thousand.
Serial letters:
        A—A (first series traced from A01A
        dated 16 June 1955)   20·00   10·00
        B—A, C—A   *each* 18·00   9·00
        D—A (last series traced
        dated 20 September 1956)   20·00   10·00

1957 (21 February) FIVE POUNDS
Designed by Stephen Gooden, R.A., featuring on the obverse the
helmeted head of Britannia, and on the reverse the lion and key.
Plate-printed in sheets of 21 at St. Luke's Works, London, on banknote
paper manufactured by Portals Ltd. with watermark incorporating the
helmeted head of Britannia. (Britannia) Five Pound notes measure
160 × 90 mm (6¼ × 3½ in.) and were legal tender until 27 June 1967.

Price

EF   VF

B277 £5   Blue, pale green and orange
Prefix coding: Letter, number, number.
Quantity printed: Not known.
Serial letters:
        A— (first series traced from A01)   11·00   8·00
        B—, C—, D—, E—   *each* 10·00   7·50
        H— (last series traced to H67)   10·00   7·50

B277/279

Reverse of B277

	EF	VF

B278 £5 Blue, pale green and orange replacement
note
Prefix coding: Letter, number, number.
Quantity printed: Not known.
Serial letter:
    M——   15·00   9·00

1961 (12 July) FIVE POUNDS
Design, watermark and dimensions as B277 above, except that £5 symbols on the reverse are printed in outline only instead of shaded in dark blue. Printed at Bank of England Works, Loughton, Essex.

	Price	
	EF	VF

B279 £5 Blue, pale green and orange
Prefix coding: Letter, number, number.
Quantity printed: Not known.
Serial letters:
    H—— (first series traced from H58),
    J——, K—— (last series traced to K45)   *each* 10·00   7·50
It will be noticed that serial numbers of B277 and B279 overlap in the H—— series.

B280 £5 Blue, pale green and orange
Prefix coding: Letter, number, number.
Quantity printed: Not known.
Serial letter:
    M——   15·00   9·00

Strictly speaking B279 and B280 belong to the Second Period of O'Brien. However, it was thought more logical to place them here.
For classification of specimen notes and errors *see* page 102.

O'BRIEN *(contd.)*

SECOND (Portrait) PERIOD (1960–62)

On 19 November 1959 the Bank of England announced that a new £1 note, bearing for the first time a portrait of the reigning monarch, would be issued in 1960. This was to be the first of a series of new designs for denominations up to £10.

The £1 and 10s. notes, which were designed by Professor Robert Austin, R.A., incorporate the Queen's portrait in a complex blend of machine-engraved geometric patterns and, on the reverse, the figure of Britannia seated. The notes were initially plate-printed in sheets of 24 at the Bank of England Works, Loughton, Essex, on banknote paper manufactured by Portals Ltd. with watermark of a continuous laureate head. However, from early 1963 printing was done on a reel-fed machine (known as "The Web"). Experimental £1 notes from this machine were put into circulation during the summar and autumn of 1961. To identify them from the general issue they carried the small capital letter "R" on the reverse and the serial prefix A—N (*see* B283). PORTRAIT £1 notes (as they are usually termed by collectors; the official title is Series C) measure 151 × 72 mm (6 × 2¾ in.) and were still legal tender when this book went to press. The 10s. notes, which measure 140 × 66 mm (5½ × 2⅝ in.), were legal tender until 22 November 1970.

1960 (17 March) ONE POUND
Design, watermark and dimensions as detailed above.

			Price	
---	---	---	EF	VF
B281	£1	Green		
		Prefix coding: Letter, number, number.		
		Quantity printed: 1782 million.		
		Serial letters:		
		A— (first series traced from A01)	5·00	2·50

B282

Common reverse of £1 O'Brien to Page

	EF	VF
B—, C—, D—, E—, H—, J—, K—, L—, N—, R—, S—, T—, U—, W—, X—, Y— *each*	4·00	2·00
Z— (last series traced to Z81)	4·00	2·50

B282 £1   Green
Prefix coding: Number, number, letter.
Quantity printed: 1782 million.
Serial letters:

—A (first series traced from 03A)	5·00	2·50
—B, —C, —D, —E, —H, —J, —K, —L, —N, —R, —S, —T, —U, —W, —X, —Y *each*	4·00	2·00
—Z (last series traced to 99Z)	4·00	2·50

B283 £1   Green
Prefix coding: Letter, number, number,
letter ("R" reverse).
Quantity printed: 6 million
Serial letters:

A—N (series traced in A01N, A05N and A06N only)	90·00	from 35·00

B283 showing position of "R" on reverse. The "G" variety found on
B292 and subsequent notes is also in this position.

O'BRIEN (contd.)

Notes with A01N have a long tail to the "R", whereas those with A05N and A06N have a short-tailed "R". So far no trace has been found of notes with the prefix A02N, A03N and A04N, which were probably printed but not put into general circulation.

		Price	
		EF	*VF*

B284 **£1**   Green
Prefix coding: Letter, number, number, letter.
Quantity printed: 76 million.
Serial letters:
B—N (series traced from B01N to
B76N)   12·00   4·00

B285 **£1**   Green replacement note
Prefix coding: Letter, number, number.
Quantity printed: 66 million.
Serial letter:
M— (series traced from M01 to M66).   8·50   4·00

1961 (12 October) TEN SHILLINGS
Design, watermark and dimensions as detailed above.

B286 **10s.**   Red-brown
Prefix coding: Letter, number, number.
Quantity printed: 756 million.
Serial letters:
A— (first series traced from A01)   5·00   2·50
B—, C—, D—, E—, H—, J—   *each* 4·00   2·00
K— (last series traced to K63)   5·00   2·50

B286

Reverse of B286

EF   VF

B287 10s.   Red-brown replacement note
        Prefix coding: Letter, number, number.
        Quantity printed: 18 million.
        Serial letter:
           M— (series traced from M01 to M18) 20·00   5·00

The £5 notes of this period (B279 and B280) can be found on page 75.
For classification of specimen notes and errors *see* page 102.

---

6. Jasper Quintus Hollom (1962–66)

Born 1917. Entered Bank service 1936. Chief Cashier 1962. Director from 1966. Deputy Governor 1970.

1963 (27 February) ONE POUND
    Design, watermark and dimensions as for L. K. O'Brien portrait notes.
    Printed on continuous reel-fed machines at the Bank of England Works,
    Loughton, Essex. Some notes (B292 and B293) carry the small capital
    letter "G" on the reverse to indicate they were printed on a Gobel
    machine.

B288

		Price	
		EF	*VF*

B288 £1 Green
Prefix coding: Letter, number, number, letter.
Quantity printed: 5875 million.
Serial letters:

	EF	*VF*
B—N (first series traced from B77N)	14·00	7·00
C—N, D—N, E—N, H—N, J—N, K—N, L—N,	each 4·00	2·00
A—R, B—R, C—R, D—R, E—R, H—R, J—R, K—R, L—R	each 4·00	2·00
A—S, B—S, C—S, D—S, E—S, H—S, J—S, K—S, L—S	each 4·00	2·00
A—T, B—T, C—T, E—T, H—T, J—T, K—T, L—T	each 4·00	2·00
A—U, B—U, C—U, D—U, E—U, H—U, J—U, K—U, L—U	each 4·00	2·00
A—W, B—W, D—W, E—W, H—W, J—W, K—W, L—W	each 4·00	2·00
A—X, B—X, C—X, D—X, E—X, H—X, J—X, K—X	each 4·00	2·00
A—Y	each 4·00	2·00
B—Y (last series traced to B10Y)	10·00	4·00

B289 £1 Green replacement note
Prefix coding: Letter, number, number.
Quantity printed: 32 million.
Serial letter:

	EF	*VF*
M— (series traced from M68 to M99)	10·00	5·00

B290 £1 Green replacement note
Prefix coding: Number, number, letter.
Quantity printed: 99 million.
Serial letter:

	EF	*VF*
—M (series traced from 01M to 99M)	10·00	5·00

B291 £1 Green replacement note
Prefix coding: Letter, number, number, letter.
Quantity printed: 8 million.
Serial letters:

	EF	*VF*
M—R (series traced from M01R to M08R)	10·00	5·00

B292 £1 Green (printed on a Gobel machine)
Prefix coding: Letter, number, number, letter ("G" reverse; *see* illustration page 77).

	EF	VF

Quantity printed: 387 million.
Serial letters:
    A—N (first series traced from A09N)   8·50   3·50
    D—T,
    C—W,
    L—X (last series traced to L99X)   *each* 6·00   3·00

B293 £1 Green replacement note (printed on a Gobel machine)
Prefix coding: Letter, number, number,
letter ("G" reverse).
Quantity printed: 28 million.
Serial letters:
    M—N (series traced from M01N to
    M28N)   10·00   5·00

1963 (4 April) TEN SHILLINGS
Design, watermark and dimensions as for L. K. O'Brien portrait notes.
Printed on continuous reel-fed machines at the Bank of England Works,
Loughton, Essex.

	Price	
	EF	VF

B294 10s. Red-brown
Prefix coding: Letter, number, number.
Quantity printed: 1025 million.
Serial letters:
    K— (first series traced from K65)   4·50   3·00
    L—, N—, R—, S—, T—, U—, W—,
    X—, Y—   *each* 3·00   2·00
    Z— (last series traced to Z96)   3·50   2·00

B295 10s. Red-brown
Prefix coding: Number, number, letter.
Quantity printed: 1015 million.
Serial letters:
    —A (first series traced from 01A)   4·50   3·00

B295

HOLLOM (contd.)

		Price	
		EF	VF
—B, —C, —D, —E, —H, —J, —K,			
—L, —N		*each* 3·00	2·00
—R (last series traced to 23R)		8·50	3·00

B296 10s.   Red-brown replacement note
Prefix coding: Letter, number, number.
Quantity printed: 34 million.
Serial letter:
   M— (series traced from M19 to M52)   15·00   5·00

1963 (21 February) FIVE POUNDS
Designed by Reynolds Stone, C.B.E., R.D.I., and of similar appearance to
the £1 and 10s. notes, featuring the Queen's portrait on the obverse, and
the figure of a child Britannia (modelled by the artist's daughter) on the
reverse. Plate-printed in sheets of 21 at the Bank of England Works,
Loughton, Essex, on banknote paper manufactured by Portals Ltd., with
watermark of a continuous laureate head. Portrait £5 notes measure
140 × 84 mm (5½ × 3$\frac{5}{16}$ in.) and were legal tender until 31 August 1973.

		Price	
		EF	VF
B297 £5 Blue			

Prefix coding: Letter, number, number.
Quantity printed: 1007 million.
Serial letters:

		EF	VF
A— (first series traced from A01)		12·00	7·50
B—, C—, D—, E—, H—, J—, K—,			
L—, N—		*each* 8·50	7·00
R— (last series traced to R16)		10·00	7·50

B297

Reverse of B297

B298 £5   Blue replacement note
Prefix coding: Letter, number, number.
Quantity printed: Not known.
Serial letter:
      M—— (series traced from M01 to M16)   12·00   7·50

1964 (21 February) TEN POUNDS
    Designed by Reynolds Stone, C.B.E., R.D.I., featuring the Queen's portrait
on the obverse together with a figure of Britannia seated; and on the
reverse a lion holding a key with the words "Ten Pounds" in a scroll
issuing from its mouth. Plate-printed in sheets of 15 at the Bank of
England Works, Loughton, Essex, on banknote paper manufactured by
Portals Ltd., with watermark of the Queen's head. Portrait £10 notes
measure 150 × 93 mm ($5\frac{7}{8}$ × $3\frac{5}{8}$ in.) and were still legal tender when this
book went to press.

B299

HOLLOM (contd.)

B299 common reverse to £10 between Hollom and Page

		Price	
		EF	VF

B299 £10 Brown
Prefix coding: Letter, number, number.
Quantity printed: Not known.
Serial letter:
A— (series traced from A01)   18·00   13·00

B300 £10 Brown replacement note
Prefix coding: Letter, number, number.
Quantity printed: Not known.
Serial letter:
M— (series traced in M01 only)   18·00   13·00

For classification of specimen notes and errors *see* page 102.

---

7. John Standish Fforde (1966–70)

Born 1921. Entered Bank service 1957. Chief Cashier 1966. Director 1970.

1967 (15 February) ONE POUND
Design, watermark and dimensions as for L. K. O'Brien portrait notes. Printed on continuous reel-fed machines at the Bank of England Works, Loughton, Essex. By 1968 existing serial letter combinations (type 1, using the second half of the alphabet N to Z as the control) had been exhausted, so the Bank began using (type 2) the first half of the alphabet A to L as the control letter (N—A, R—A, S—A and so on). Some notes carry the small capital letter "G" on the reverse to indicate they were printed on a Gobel machine.

B301

			Price	
			EF	VF

B301 £1 Green
Prefix coding: Letter, number, number,
 letter (type 1).
Quantity printed: 1475 million.
Serial letters:

	EF	VF
B—Y (first series traced from B11Y)	8·00	4·00
C—Y, D—Y, H—Y, J—Y, K—Y, L—Y *each* 4·00		2·50
A—Z, B—Z, C—Z, D—Z, E—Z, H—Z, J—Z, L—Z *each* 4·00		2·50

B302 £1 Green replacement note
Prefix coding: Letter, number, number,
 letter (type 1).
Quantity printed: 38 million.
Serial letters:
  M—R (series traced from M09R to M47R)8·00   4·00

B303 £1 Green (printed on a Gobel machine)
Prefix coding: Letter, number, number,
 letter (type 1) ("G" reverse)
Quantity printed: 198 million.
Serial letters:
  E—Y, K—Z   *each* 6·00   3·00

B304 £1 Green replacement note (printed on a Gobel machine)
Prefix coding: Letter, number, number,
 letter (type 1) ("G" reverse).
Quantity printed: 5 million.
Serial letters:
  M—N (series traced from M29N to
  M34N)   12·00   6·00

B305 £1 Green
Prefix coding: Letter, number, number,
 letter (type 2).
Quantity printed: 4000 million (estimated).

FFORDE (*contd.*)

		Price	
		EF	VF

Serial letters:

	EF	VF
N—A (first series traced from N—A)	3·50	2·00
N—B, N—C, N—D, N—E, N—H, N—J, N—K, N—L	*each* 3·00	2·00
R—A, R—C, R—D, R—E, R—H, R—J, R—K	*each* 3·00	2·00
S—A, S—B, S—C, S—D, S—E, S—H, S—J, S—K, S—L	*each* 3·00	2·00
T—A, T—B, T—C, T—D, T—E, T—H, T—J, T—K, T—L	*each* 3·00	2·00
U—A, U—B, U—C, U—D	*each* 3·00	2·00
W—A, W—B, W—C	*each* 3·00	2·00
X—B, X—C (last series traced to X41C)	*each* 3·00	2·00

B306 £1   Green replacement note
Prefix coding: Letter, number, number, letter (type 2)
Quantity printed: 300 million (estimated).
Serial letters:

	EF	VF
R—M (series traced from R01M), S—M	*each* 4·00	2·00
T—M, U—M	*each* 5·00	2·00

£1 notes bearing the signatures of J. S. Fforde and J. B. Page with consecutive serial numbers are available (EF) at £15 a pair.

		Price	
		EF	VF

B307 £1   Green (printed on a Gobel machine)
Prefix coding: Letter, number, number, letter (type 2).
Quantity printed: 250 million (estimated).
Serial letters:

	EF	VF
R—B, R—L, U—E	*each* 5·00	2·50

B308 £1   Green replacement note (Printed on a Gobel machine)
Prefix coding: Letter, number, number, letter (type 2).
Quantity printed: 100 million (estimated).
Serial letters:

	EF	VF
N—M	5·00	2·50
T—M	10·00	5·00

The T—M prefix is found both with and without "G" reverse, *see* B306 above.

B310

1967 (15 February) TEN SHILLINGS
Design, watermark and dimensions as for L. K. O'Brien notes of the
Second Period. Printed on continuous reel-fed machines at the Bank
of England Works, Loughton, Essex.

			Price	
			EF	*VF*
B309	10s.	Red-brown.		
		Prefix coding: Number, number, letter.		
		Quantity printed: 768 million.		
		Serial letters:		
		—R (first series traced from 26R)	5·00	2·00
		—S, —T, —U, —W, —X, —Y *each*	3·00	1·50
		—Z (last series traced to 94Z)	4·50	2·00
B310	10s.	Red-brown		
		Prefix coding: Letter, number, number, letter.		
		Quantity printed: 335 million.		
		Serial letters:		
		A—N (first series traced from A01N),		
		B—N, C—N, D—N (last series traced to D38N) *each*	3·00	1·50
B311	10s.	Red-brown replacement note		
		Prefix coding: Letter, number, number.		
		Quantity printed: 25 million.		
		Serial letter:		
		M— (series traced from M56 to M80)	5·00	3·00

1967 (9 January) FIVE POUNDS
Design, watermark and dimensions as for J. Q. Hollom notes. Printed at
the Bank of England Works, Loughton.

FFORDE (*contd.*)

B314

| | | Price | |
| | | EF | VF |

B312 £5 Blue
Prefix coding: Letter, number, number.
Quantity printed: 775 million.
Serial letters:

	EF	VF
R— (first series traced from R20)	10·00	7·50
S—, T—, U—, W—, X—, Y—, Z—		
(last series traced to Z99)	*each* 8·50	7·00

B313 £5 Blue replacement note
Prefix coding: Letter, number, number.
Quantity printed: Not known.
Serial letter:

	EF	VF
M— (series traced from M18 to M38)	12·00	7·50

B314 £5 Blue
Prefix coding: Number, number, letter.
Quantity printed: 850 million (including B323).
Serial letters:

	EF	VF
—A (first series traced from 01A)	9·00	7·00
—B, —C, —D, —E, —H, —J, —K,		
—L (last series traced to 40L)	*each* 8·00	7·00

B315 £5 Blue replacement note
Prefix coding: Number, number, letter.
Quantity printed: 15 million (including B324)
Serial letter:

	EF	VF
—M (series traced from 01M to 15M)	10·00	7·50

£5 notes bearing the signatures of J. S. Fforde and J. B. Page with consecutive serial numbers are available (EF) at £20 a pair.

B316

1967 (9 January) TEN POUNDS
Design, watermark and dimensions as for J. Q. Hollom notes. Printed at
the Bank of England Works, Loughton.

		Price	
		EF	VF
B316 £10	Brown *Prefix coding:* Letter, number, number. *Quantity printed:* Not known. *Serial letter:*		
	A— (series traced from A01)	16·50	12·00
B317 £10	Brown replacement note *Prefix coding:* Letter, number, number. *Quantity printed:* under 1 million. *Serial letter:*		
	M— (series traced in M01 only)	18·50	13·50

£10 notes bearing the signatures of J. S. Fforde and J. B. Page with consecutive serial numbers are available (EF) at £30 a pair.

1970 (9 July) TWENTY POUNDS
Designed by Harry Eccleston as the first of the new PICTORIAL series (official title: Series D). The obverse features the Queen's portrait, the reverse
the statue of Shakespeare from Kent Memorial in Westminster Abbey
and a scene from Romeo and Juliet. Plate-printed in sheets of 15 at the
Bank of England Works, Loughton, Essex, on banknote paper manufactured by Portals Ltd. with watermark of the Queen's head. Twenty
pound notes measure 160 × 90 mm ($6\frac{5}{16} × 3\frac{9}{16}$ in.) and were still legal
tender when this book went to press. (Although the first series of notes
was signed by J. S. Fforde, he had, in fact, ceased to be Chief Cashier in
March 1970.)

FFORDE (*contd.*)

B318

B318 common reverse to £20 between Fforde and Page

                                                         Price

                                           EF   *VF*

B318 £20   Multicoloured (purple predominating)
              Prefix coding: Letter, number, number.
              Quantity printed: Under 1 million.
              Serial letter:
                  A— (series traced in A01 only)   30·00   25·00

B319 £20   Multicoloured replacement note
              Prefix coding: Letter, number, number.
              Quantity printed: Not known.
              Serial letter:
                  M— (series traced in M01 only)   35·00   25·00

For classification of specimen notes and errors *see* page 102.

8. John Brangwyn Page (1970—)

Born 1924. Entered Bank service 1948. Assistant Chief Cashier 1966. First deputy Chief Cashier 1968. Chief Cashier from 1 March 1970.

PORTRAIT SERIES

1971 (date unknown) ONE POUND
Design, watermark and dimensions as for L. K. O'Brien portrait notes. Printed on continuous reel-fed machines at the Bank of England Works, Loughton, Essex. (£1 notes bearing the signature of J. B. Page were issued concurrently with those of J. S. Fforde for two years with many serial prefixes shared by both cashiers.)

			Price	
			EF	*VF*
B320	£1	Green		
		Prefix coding: Letter, number, number, letter.		
		Quantity printed: 3900 million (estimated)		
		Serial letters:		
		S—L (first series, traced in S87L, S89L and S90L only)	10·00	4·00
		T—B, T—D, T—E, T—H, T—K, T—L	*each* 2·00	†
		U—A, U—B, U—C, U—D, U—H	*each* 2·00	†
		W—A, W—B, W—C, W—D, W—E, W—H	*each* 2·00	†
		X—A, X—B, X—C, X—D, X—E, X—H, X—J, X—K, X—L	*each* 2·00	†
		Y—A, Y—B, Y—C, Y—D, Y—E, Y—H, Y—J, Y—K, Y—L	*each* 2·00	†
		Z—A, Z—B, Z—C, Z—D, Z—E, Z—H, Z—J, Z—K, Z—L	*each* 2·00	†

B320

PAGE (contd.)

Price

EF   VF

B321 £1   Green replacement note
          Prefix coding: Letter, number, number,
              letter.
          Quantity printed: Not yet complete.
          Serial letters:
              R—M (first series traced from R47M)   5·00   2·50
              S—M, W—M, X—M   *each* 3·00   †
              (Y—M and Z—M not yet traced)

£1 notes with consecutive serial numbers bearing the signatures of J. B. Page and J. S. Fforde are available EF at £12 a pair.

By mid-1973, the existing serial combinations were almost used up, and the Bank of England introduced the serial prefix letter, letter, number number for the first time.

Price

EF   VF

B322 £1   Green
          Prefix coding: Letter, letter, number,
              number.
          Quantity printed: Not yet complete.
          Serial letters:
              AN— (first series traced from AN01),
              BN—   2·50   †
              AR—, BR—, AU—, BU—   2·00   †
              AS—, BS—, AW—, BW—   2·00   †
              AT—, BT—, AX—, BX—   2·00   †

B323 £1   Green replacement note
          Prefix coding: Letter, letter, number,
              number.
          Quantity printed: Not yet complete.
          Serial letters:
              MR— (first series traced from MR01),
              MS—   2·50   †

B322

B324

1971 (date unknown) FIVE POUNDS
Design, watermark and dimensions as for J. Q.
Hollom notes. Printed at the Bank of England
Works, Loughton, Essex. (Five pound notes bearing
the signature of J. B. Page were issued concurrently
with those of J. S. Fforde for two years with some
serial prefixes shared by both cashiers.)

			Price	
			EF	VF
B324 £5	Blue			
	Prefix coding: Number, number, letter.			
	Quantity printed: 850 million (including B314).			
	Serial letters:			
	—C, —D, —E, —H, —J, —K, —L *each*	8·00	6·50
B325 £5	Blue replacement note			
	Prefix coding: Number, number, letter.			
	Quantity printed: 15 million (including B315).			
	Serial letter:			
	—M (series traced from 04M)	10·00	7·00

£5 notes bearing the signatures of J. B. Page and J. S. Fforde with consecutive serial numbers are available (EF) at £18 a pair.

1971 (date unknown) TEN POUNDS
Design, watermark and dimensions as for J. Q. Hollom notes. Printed at
the Bank of England Works, Loughton, Essex.

B326 £10 Brown
Prefix coding: Letter, number, number.

B326

Price

EF   VF

Quantity printed: 250 million (estimated).
Serial letters:
B— (first series traced from B01),
C—, D—   *each* 15·00   12·00

B327 £10 Brown replacement note
Prefix coding: Letter, number, number.
Quantity printed: 20 million (estimated)
Serial letter:
M—   17·00   14·00

£10 notes bearing the signatures of J. B. Page and J. S. Fforde with consecutive serial numbers are available (EF) at £30 a pair.

For classification of specimen notes and errors *see* page 102.

B329

PICTORIAL SERIES

1970 (date not known) TWENTY POUNDS
Design, dimensions and watermark as for J. S. Fforde notes. Printed at the Bank of England Works, Loughton.

			Price	
			EF	VF
B328 £20	Multicoloured (purple predominating) *Prefix coding:* Letter, number, number. *Quantity printed:* Not yet complete. *Serial letters:*			
	A—		25·00	†
	B—, C—		22·00	†
B329 £20	Multicoloured replacement note *Prefix coding:* Letter, number, number *Quantity printed:* Not yet complete. *Serial letter:*			
	M—		23·00	†

1975 (20 February) TEN POUNDS
Designed by Harry Eccleston as the third in the series of Pictorial notes. The obverse features the Queen's portrait in State Robes, a medallion of Britannia and a vignette derived from the lily symbol used by Florence Nightingale. On the reverse the portrait of Florence Nightingale was created from photographs taken on her return from the Crimean War. It is set beside a vignette based on a contemporary lithograph showing her at work in the Barracks Hospital, Scutari. Plate-printed in sheets of 20 at the Bank of England Works, Loughton, Essex, on banknote paper manufactured by Portals Ltd., with watermark of Florence Nightingale's head. These notes measure 149 × 92 mm ($5\frac{7}{8}$ × $3\frac{5}{16}$ in.) and are still legal tender.

B330

PAGE (*contd.*)

Reverse of B330

		Price	
		EF	VF

B330 £10   Multicoloured (brown predominating)
Prefix coding: Letter, number, number.
Quantity printed: Not yet complete.
Serial letters:
     A— (first series traced from A01), B— 12·00   †

B331 £10   Multicoloured replacement note
Prefix coding: Letter, number, number.
Quantity printed: Not yet complete.
Serial letters:
     M— (series traced from M01)   12·00   †

1971 (11 November) FIVE POUNDS
Designed by Harry Eccleston as the second of the Pictorial series of notes. On the obverse it features the Queen's portrait, a vignette depicting a Winged Victory and a medallion of Britannia. On the reverse there is a portrait of the first Duke of Wellington and a vignette of a scene from the Peninsular War. Plate-printed in sheets of 18 at the Bank of England Works, Loughton, Essex, on banknote paper manufactured by Portals Ltd. with continuous watermark of Wellington's head. "Wellington" £5 notes measure 145 × 77 mm ($5\frac{3}{4}$ × $3\frac{1}{16}$ in.) and were still legal tender when this book went to press. Due to difficulties of production, a different printing process was adopted in 1973 and the new notes appeared with a small capital "L" on the reverse (meaning Litho).

B332 £5   Multicoloured (pale blue predominating)
Prefix coding: Letter, number, number.
Quantity printed: Not yet complete.

B332

Reverse of B332

	EF	VF
Serial letters:		
A— (first series traced from A01)	7·50	†
B—, C—, D—, E—, H—, J—, K—, L—	*each* 6·00	†

Possibly more letters.

Reverse of B334

PAGE *(contd.)*   *Price*

                                                        EF   VF

B333 £5   Multicoloured replacement note
            Prefix coding: Letter, number, number.
            Quantity printed: Not yet complete.
            Serial letters:
                M— (series traced from M01)   7·50   †

1973 (August) FIVE POUNDS
    Design, dimensions and watermark as for B331 above, but note carries
    small capital letter "L" on the reverse to the right of the £5
    denomination, to indicate it was printed by lithography. It is also dis-
    tinguished by a different serial prefix: Number, number, letter.

                                                        Price

                                                        EF   VF

B334 £5   Multicoloured (pale blue predominating)
            Prefix coding: Number, number, letter.
            Quantity printed: Not yet complete.
            Serial letters:
                —A (first series traced from 08A), —B,
                —C, —D, —E, —H, —J, —K, —L *each* 6·00   †
B335 £5   Multicoloured replacement note
            Prefix coding: Number, number, letter.
            Quantity printed: Not yet complete.
            Serial letter:
                —M   6·50   †

    The Bank of England have stated their intention of issuing a new £1 note
in due course, but this is not expected for several years.

Information for the New Collector

Forming a Collection

Don't be too concerned about obtaining older notes in perfect condition. Only a handful of perfect Bank of England notes, issued up to the turn of the century, now exist, and these notes are acceptable in almost any condition. Naturally, modern notes should be collected in at least EF (extremely fine) condition where possible. However, this is not always possible and many notaphilists are happy to put aside VF (very fine) notes of, say, Hollom from circulation, which although recent are already scarce, replacing them with better examples when they come along.

Badly creased and dirty notes can benefit by soaking and then pressing them between heavy books, but generally speaking it is better, as with stamps, to leave them alone; cleaning with washing-up liquids, etc., adversely affects the notaphilic value, while ironing produces an artificial sheen which destroys much of their value to the collector.

Notes can be mounted in specially made albums (including the Stanley Gibbons). A type that has much to recommend it is the Hagner: this album has its pages already divided to accommodate the usual sizes of English notes. The pockets of crystal clear sheeting contain black card, which enhances the appearance of the notes, and are open at the top. Many collectors prefer this type to the floppy vinyl pockets opening from the side which are used by other makers.

There are many ways of forming a collection, ranging from the "one of each" type of collection to specialisation in low serial numbers—particularly the "A" series (A01A 000001), same number serials (M23L 555555), and one of each serial prefix of a particular Cashier, i.e. A . . ., B . . ., C . . ., D . . . etc.

Design

Because the security of a banknote depends on a multiplicity of features a variety of arts and crafts are used in design. Many different artists work on a banknote. In 1940 a metal filament was added to banknotes, the invention of Mr. S. B. Chamberlain, General Manager of the Bank's printing works.

Dates

No modern Bank of England notes are dated. Until the introduction of the
10s. note in 1928 (B210) all notes were dated. The last dated notes were the
white £5 notes of 1956 (B276).

Notes were not necessarily issued in the year that they were dated. Notes
dated 1956 were still being issued in 1957. Many earlier notes were not
issued at all during the year for which they were dated. This was because
the Bank of England have always stockpiled notes to ensure a sufficient
supply for any contingency. The fluctuations of demand for notes can be
quite marked, particularly at times like Christmas.

This led to a unique situation with the new £20 note issued in 1970
(B318). It is the first note signed by a Chief Cashier (Fforde) who was not in
office when the note was issued. Between the printing and stockpiling of
the note he had been promoted and a new Chief Cashier (Page) appointed.

Printing

At any given time there are more than 1500 million banknotes in circulation. The 1974 figures were £20: 19 million; £10: 81 million; £5: 602
million; £1: 883 million. There are still 25 million 10s. notes outstanding.

The average life of a £1 note is now about 10 months and of a £5 is 15
months.

From 1791 all Bank of England notes were printed on their own
premises, St. Luke's Printing Works in London, until larger premises were
needed in 1956. New printing works, specially designed, occupying half a
million square feet of floor space, were constructed at Loughton, Essex,
and about 2000 people are employed there.

Until about 1961 all notes were sheet-fed printed. Sheets of paper were
large enough for twenty-four £1 notes. Sheets were stacked and stored so
that the ink could dry before the next stage of the printing was undertaken.
Several printing processes were needed, and the whole operation of
printing a banknote could take weeks.

In 1961 the Bank experimented with various machines and developed a
reel-fed process in which the notes were printed in one continuous
operation.

Reels of paper two miles long are used. This has meant that watermarks
can no longer be perfectly matched to the paper, as could be achieved with
sheet-fed printing, and continuous watermarks were designed to meet the
difficulty of a "sheet" two miles long.

The quantity of notes printed in any given issue has been calculated on
the basis of one million for each of the serial prefixes 01–99 (100,000 for
white £5 notes). It is, however, by no means certain that each series was
completed or, if it was, that it was actually issued. Each series has been

checked against actual notes, and the earliest and latest serial number has been recorded. The absence or omission of various prefixes and numbers merely indicates the limit of sampling to date, and additions or corrections will appear in future catalogues.

Replacement Notes

A replacement note is used by the Bank of England to make up a bundle where one or more notes may have been damaged. At various points in the production run, a note from a bundle bearing a different serial prefix from the series in progress is inserted. As printing has become more highly complex, so the rate of faulty notes has increased, but even so it is still a minute fraction of the total.

Only the Bank of England can positively identify a replacement note, but although most of the replacement serials are now known, it is essential with present-day issues to preserve the note buttressed on each side by notes from the normal series. This is because replacement serials are often released in blocks for general circulation, especially at the end of a run.

The following serial prefixes are known to have been used for replacements:

Cashier	10s.	£1	£1 ("G" reverse)
K. O. Peppiatt (threaded)	—A	S—S	
P. S. Beale	—A	S—S	
L. K. O'Brien	—A	S—S	
		S—T	
L. K. O'Brien (portrait)	M—	M—	
J. Q. Hollom	M—	M—	M—N
		—M	
		M—R	
J. S. Fforde	M—	M—R	M—N
		R—M	N—M
		S—M	T—M
		T—M	
		U—M	
J. B. Page		R—M	
		S—M	
		W—M	
		X—M	
		M—R	
		M—S	

All higher denomination notes in the portrait series are replaced by notes with the prefix M— (and in the case of Fforde and Page £5 notes by —M also).

Opinion is divided as to the existence of a recognisable replacement system before the Second World War. Nothing has come to light to prove or disprove the various serial letters suggested, and the Bank of England are not prepared to confirm or deny the existence of replacement notes during this period.

In Treasury notes, the odd letter out is Z, which was used to prefix the bottom right-hand note of each sheet of £1 notes (but not 10s. notes) from the Third Issue onwards. While Z prefix notes of Bradbury and Fisher are therefore slightly more rare, there is nothing to suggest they were deliberately set aside as replacements and may have acted rather as "control" notes.

Serial Letters

With the exception of the letters I and Q, Treasury notes are found with serial letters from every letter in the alphabet, starting with A and ending with Z.

The Bank of England make a rather more selective use of the alphabet. In the £1 and 10s. issues of C. P. Mahon and B. S. Catterns, all letters of the alphabet were used, except for I, P and Q. Later the letters F, G and V were omitted, giving a conveniently round figure of 20 letters available for each issue. When the portrait notes were introduced in 1960, the letter O was dropped and M was set aside for replacements.

Errors and Specimens

With the exception of the modern portrait £1 notes of Fforde and Page, and the £5 Wellington notes, errors are relatively scarce and in pre-war Bank of England and Treasury notes extremely rare. Because of this it is difficult to put an exact price on every single type of error that can occur.

However, the following classification deals with most of the relevant errors, and a *minimum* price is quoted (i.e. that which might be asked for a modern portrait note). As a rough guide, collectors should expect to pay double these prices for errors on post-war Britannia notes, a premium of 50% for pre-war notes and treble the prices below for Treasury note errors (except specimens). The prices below are for 10s. and £1 notes only; higher denominations would be treated pro rata.

Conversely specimen notes are generally found only in the earlier notes, though any specimen is extremely rare. Modern Bank of England practice is to release photographs only of specimen notes.

Error category D: different serial numbers on same note

Error category K: extra paper through faulty folding

For the purpose of quotation the original catalogue number together with the suffix should be cited:

A.	Specimen notes, overprinted SPECIMEN and generally numbered Aoo oooooo, Qoo oooooo (wartime issues), or Roo oooooo (post-war Britannia notes)	from £90
B.	Serial numbers missing top and bottom	from £25
C.	One serial number missing (or partly missing)	from £15
D.	Top serial number different from bottom (Portrait notes)	from £6
E.	Identical serial numbers on a pair of notes	from £15 the pair
F.	Identical but different serial numbers top and bottom on a pair of notes	from £25 the pair
G.	Note printed on one side only	from £20
H.	Part of design omitted	from £10
J.	Double or faulty printing	from £8
K.	Extra paper, through faulty folding	from £10

Collectors are invited to submit details of any other type of error note in which they are specifically interested.

Paper

The first notes of the Bank of England were written by hand on ordinary paper purchased from stationers. Forgery led the Bank to experiment with marbled paper which could be matched exactly to a counterfoil, and in 1697 watermarked paper was used. Linen rag and cotton was mixed to make the paper.

In 1724 Henry Portal of Whitchurch, Hampshire, became the paper supplier to the Bank of England, and that firm is to this day the Bank's supplier.

No one is allowed to use the special watermarked paper used for Bank of England notes, or paper with a similar watermark.

Growth in Demand for Notes

In the early days of the Bank of England, the demand for notes was small enough to permit a somewhat slow process of production. In 1783 the banknote paper was sent in large iron-bound chests by wagon from the paper makers. Each month a supply of paper was then sent to George Cole, who had succeeded James Cole in 1748 as printer for the Bank of England (his business was at The Crown, Great Kirby Street, Hatton Garden). Then every morning the engraved copper plates were drawn from the Treasury in the Bank and taken to the printer where a clerk counted the sheets as they came off the press.

In 1791 Cole's business was transferred to the Bank, and at that time daily output was around 2000 notes. By 1800 there was a growing demand for £1 and £2 notes and some 15,000 notes were printed daily. This doubled by 1805.

By 1966 the daily output of banknotes was eight million, most of them being £1 and 10s. notes. Ten shilling notes were less in demand and at one time the ratio was one 10s. note to every seven £1 notes. The average life of banknotes of low denomination is only a few months. This short life for the 10s. (as well as advancing inflation) was one reason for making the 50p a coin and not a note on decimalisation in 1971.

By 1974 the daily output of banknotes had fallen to six million, but the face value had greatly increased due to inflation. And the once rarely seen £5 is rapidly overtaking the £1 as the most widely used note in circulation.

Mutilated Notes

Until 1928 registers were kept of all Bank of England notes so that at any time the Bank knew not only how much was outstanding, but which actual notes they were. The volume of modern paper money is such that registers are no longer practical.

The registers are still kept for the old White notes of £10 and higher denominations. In the past it has meant that the Bank could replace lost or stolen notes (given certain guarantees against the notes turning up), as well as badly mutilated notes.

Some five million mutilated notes are dealt with annually.

Old Notes not yet Redeemed at end of February 1968

£1000	63 notes
£500	78 notes
£100	4910 notes
£50	5540 notes
£20	7800 notes

In view of the greatly increased notaphilic interest and values, the Bank of England have declined to give later figures to prevent undue speculation.

Forgeries

It is an offence for anyone to purchase, receive from any person, or have in his custody or possession a forged banknote knowing it to be forged regardless of its age or country of origin. Forged notes are, in fact, immediately confiscated. It is also illegal to photograph or photocopy a Bank of England note without the express authority of the Bank of England.

How to Grade Condition

Unlike postage stamps, which are usually collected only in perfect condition, banknotes are collectable in various stages of wear and tear. This is because, at times, banknotes were officially cut in half for transport security reasons—the two halves going by separate transport and being joined at the bank of destination; other notes were made to do service for as long as thirty years and none was preserved in uncirculated condition. Rare notes, such as running cash notes, would be acceptable to collectors in very dirty and torn state. This does not, of course, apply to modern banknotes which should be collected in at least VF (very fine) condition.

The new collector can quickly establish the condition of a banknote by using the table below. The basic conditions are:

UNC	uncirculated	100
EF	extremely fine	90
VF	very fine	75
F	fine	55
Fair	fair	30

Table of Damage Numbers

Cleanliness:

Just detectable soiling	5
Considerable soiling and/or bankers' marks	10
Very dirty note with legibility considerably reduced	20

Folding:

One or two folds that leave only a just-detectable crease	5
Several folds which are clearly visible	10
Many and repeated folds	20

Surface:

Detectable damage to surface	5
Damage to surface at several places or over considerable area	10
Considerable damage to surface over extended areas	20

Edges:

Just detectable roughness or indentation of edges ..	5
Considerable damage to edges and/or tears not extending beyond margin of note	10
Badly damaged edges, or tears extending into design of note	20

Body:

One or two pin holes	5
Several pin holes, or one or two larger holes	10
Several larger holes	20

As an example let us consider a note which is slightly soiled, has a number of firm folds, an undamaged surface, slightly damaged edges and a pin hole or two. The five damage numbers would be:

Cleanliness	5
Folding	10
Surface	0
Edges	5
Body	5
Total	**25**

This total is subtracted from 100, giving 75, which grades the note as VF (very fine).

The banknotes in this catalogue have been priced at EF and VF conditions from 1914 and VF before that date.

Bibliography

Few books have been written specifically on Treasury and Bank of England notes, but the following can be recommended:

Bank of England and Treasury Notes 1694–1970 by D. M. Miller (Minerva Numismatic Handbooks No. 6, published by Corbitt and Hunter Ltd., Newcastle upon Tyne, 1970).

A Guide to Collecting English Banknotes by David Bevan (published by Larson Publications, New Malden, Surrey, 1970).

The Bank of England Note by A. D. Mackenzie (published by Cambridge University Press, 1953).

There are a wide variety of books on banknote collecting in general. Particularly recommended is:

The Story of Paper Money by Yasha Beresiner and Colin Narbeth (published by David and Charles, Newton Abbot, 1973).

All aspects of banknote collecting are covered by the International Bank Note Society. Details are obtainable from the Assistant Secretary (Europe):

Mr. F. Philipson,
5 Windermere Road,
Beeston, Notts,
NG9 3AS,
England.